Ready or Not - A Disaster Survival Handbook

Ready or Not

A Disaster Survival Handbook

Authors Susan Conniry & Tom Beasley

Preparing For...

You may remember the Y2K issue. There was a major shortcoming in computer application software that on January 1, 2000 computer systems might interpret the 00 as 1900. The Y2K bug was a ticking time bomb. Companies around the world scrambled to come up with year 2000 compliant software. The time prior to the rollover was wrought with worry and uncertainty. Much was written and many hypothesized that we would need a miracle to live through the upheaval that might follow the breakdown of the computers. Hundreds of "survival" books and websites appeared and it seemed that everyone was now an "expert" on preparedness.

We were gravely concerned that the information being provided to the public was filled with inaccuracies. As such, we wrote a bi-weekly preparedness column for an internet magazine. But when the clock rolled over to January 1, 2000, no major outages were reported, airplanes still flew and the whole world went on with its normal life, our editor told us that since we had weathered the Y2K storm, there would be no need to provide further "survival tips."

However, even though Y2K turned out to be merely a drop in the bucket nothing changed the fact that we still live in a volatile environment, one that will always pose the possibility of natural and man-made disasters. And, the fact that we fixed the bug doesn't change the fact that our dependence on techology still leaves us in a vulnerable position if parts of the system fail. Couple that with our dependence on oil and the fact that we have already reached peak production and are heading down the other side of the bell curve, there are several ways that our umbilical cord may be cut. Therefore, we still need to be prudently prepared.

So if you are the type of person who believes that the responsibility for your life lies in your hands, and not those of bureaucratic agencies, then read on. For you are the Captain of your own destiny.

> Go sail your ship.

This book is dedicated to the animal in all of us; that part of us that knows instinctively how to stay alive!

Susan Conniry & Tom Beasley,
Lakeside, California

www.readyornotsurvival.com

copyright © 2006

Ready or Not Publishing

All rights reserved

Published by:

Ready or Not

All rights reserved. Except for use in a review, no portion of this book may be reproduced in any form without the express written permission of the publisher.

Printed & bound in the United States of America

warning
All recommendations and technical data presented here reflect the views of the authors. The information contained within this publication should be used for guidance only and approached with great caution. Information received from reading this manual and the sources recommended within it are provided "as is" and without warranty or guarantee, either expressed or implied. All implied warranties or fitness
for a particular use or purpose are hereby excluded.

The Publisher assumes no responsibility for the use or misuse of information contained within this guide. The Publisher does not advocate the breaking of laws,
or future laws.

§ | CONTENTS

Page		
11	§ i	Preface
13	§ ii	Introduction
15	§ iii	The survivalist Survival skills as a basis for preparedness
17	§ iv	Simplicity Keep it simple—needs not wants
19	§ 1	Shelter The number one priority
29	§ 2	Water More than just collection
47	§ 3	Fire We love it and we need it
59	§ 4	Food Thanks for the grub
79	§ 5	Sanitation Minimizing the risks
87	§ 6	Emergency first aid Planning your techniques
97	§ 7	Lists Focusing attention
109	§ 8	Directory Resources
113	§ 9	About the authors
115	§ 10	Note pages

Ready or Not

Preface

Unfortunately it is only when catastrophes strike, be they natural or man-made, that they show us how dependent we are and how connected we have become to the umbilical cord of society. And they reveal, too, how easily and quickly that cord can be severed, and, in the aftermath of a tragedy, how chaos and panic can swiftly permeate our lives.

Keeping things simple is not very popular these days. In this modern age of technological innovations our world has become remarkably complex. Nowhere is this more evident than in Emergency Preparedness. Hundreds of books have been written, dozens of videos and survival kits marketed, and many informative web sites created, each one more complex than the one before; each one desperate to convince the reader, viewer or buyer of the value of the product.

Yet study any one of these sources and you will find the most crucial piece of advice is missing—a statement regarding your survival priorities. Understanding your priorities in an emergency situation can mean the difference between life and death. And the simple truth is—these priorities are always the same—in any environment, in any emergency. Quite simply, you just have to ensure that your basic needs are met.

Regardless of the nature of the catastrophe, or the length of time you have to endure it, your first survival needs are always shelter, water, fire and food, in that order. All the rest are wants.

And hold this thought. You are the missing part of the survival equation. Your ability to rise to the occasion, to think outside the box, to fend for yourself, will make all the difference. Regardless of what disruptions occur, be they man-made or natural, or where you happen to be when disaster strikes, making sure your basic needs are met will diminish your fear in any survival situation and increase the likelihood of your success. Obviously your needs will be different depending on where you live. Isolated without power or water on the 20th floor of an apartment building presents practical difficulties that differ dramatically from those of a homeowner with a back yard who suffers the same depravations. But the needs are the same—it's just the remedies that differ.

This handbook provides the basics; information to enable you to meet your survival needs until society regroups and links up with you again; to provide you with the knowledge and skills to stay alive long enough for the centralized services to come back on line. Although the skills could be used for longer, and once learned will never leave you, we recommend further training before embarking upon a full survivalist lifestyle.

This book will help you meet your basic survival needs when the worst thing you can image actually happens. The information will help you to survive in the immediate aftermath of any emergency. So read it carefully, understand it and above all, practice and prepare.

And, by the way, we do practice what we preach! On October, 2003, the worst fire in the history of California ravaged San Diego County. Our home stood in its way. Practicing what we have preached and writtten about for years, we were prepared. We had cleared the brush, practiced fire drills and equipped our home with a simple misting system. As the fire approached, we turned on the misters, and evacuated. When we returned 32 hours later we found our home standing in the midst of the fire damage. Everything else was gone: outbuildings, vehicles and landscaping. We were without power for 11 days and the phones were not connected for 7 weeks, but we made it through the "dark" days. We never impacted the emergency services; we stayed home and took care of ourselves. Since then we have rebuilt our lives but we continue to be prepared in the event that another catastrophe might side swipe us. Complacency is not part of our personalities. We are survivors! You can be too.

Introduction

Our earth, unstable and unpredictable, has the potential on a daily basis to create havoc and destruction caused by natural disasters such as floods, tornadoes, hurricanes, earthquakes and volcanic eruptions, to name but a few.

Add to that the increased risks from nuclear, biological and chemical hazards. And the seemingly constant terrorist threats that assail us, whether homegrown or imported from abroad.

Note also that our frail and overburdened infrastructure is crumbling and there aren't enough funds to adequately prop it back up. Even at home, water treatment plants are failing, bridges are falling down, and antiquated sewage systems are in a state of disrepair.

Globally, we see overpopulation and famine, disasters caused by drought or widespread flooding, entire countries ravaged by disease and war, and stock markets that are as volatile as any we have ever experienced. Now we have no limit to the number and types of potential disasters that may cause death and destruction to our earth and ourselves.

Sounds terrible doesn't it?

A good point to remember here is that we have always lived with disasters. Humans have suffered at the hands of the elements and each other since time immemorial. But whether today's disasters are natural or man-made, part of our problem is that technology has lulled us into a false sense of security and we are now much less able to deal with any event that occurs out of the norm with any degree of effectiveness.

The fact is, we have become a society so ensconced in the interdependence of modern technology that we seem to have lost our personal strengths. We have abandoned nature's skill-set: self-confidence, resourcefulness and adaptability.

How has this happened?

Through a process of erosion we have neglected our mental and physical health. We no longer think for ourselves. We trust that all our needs, wants, and desires will be met as if by magic—pulled out of the hat of our modern computerized society. We assume that FEMA (Federal Emergency Management Agency) will advise us to evacuate before the hurricane hits. We believe the Red Cross will provide comforting hot coffee and a cot. We trust that the government's low interest loans will be available to us when we begin the task of rebuilding.

We have been slowly suffocating in the comfort zone. Like frogs in water, we sat complacently in the pot as the water was heated. It was comfortable while the water was warm. But man-made or natural disasters may rapidly cause the pot to boil and overflow. As we found out during the aftermath of Hurrican Katrina in 2005, we may be moments away from finding out that we are not immune to failures of technology and that government agencies, local or federal, may be ill equipped to help.

The prudent have never totally relied on governmental agencies and have always been ready and individually prepared. They are in some way conscious of the fact that society is now so interconnected that if any part of it is severed, the results could be catastrophic.

So, now you must ask yourself the important question, "Do you want to survive?" If your answer is a resounding "Yes!," read on. However, we must warn you right up front, first response survival takes energy and a positive attitude. It involves advance planning and preparedness.

Being an armchair "survivalist" would be like being an armchair pilot, you will never get off the ground.

Survival skills as a basis for preparedness

A survivalist is not someone who has stocked up on guns and gold and built an underground bunker guarded by Rottweillers. A true survivalist has acquired knowledge and learned simple skills that will enable him or her to live with the earth. This is knowledge that can never be taken away from them.

More importantly, this knowledge has displaced the fear of the unknown. It is the best insurance anyone can have, particularly if faced with natural disasters, man-made emergencies or even terrorist attacks.

Being prepared and having emergency supplies on hand in case of a disaster is sensible and we have listed essential items to keep in your survival kit in many of the chapters of this book. Though it is important, and certainly prudent, to stock up on food, water and other supplies, it is only a partial solution. To be truly prepared for changing times ahead we need a solution that goes beyond 72-hour survival packages.

This handbook is designed to provide you with enough information and genuine advice to survive a period of time during which no, or very few, emergency services or everyday utilities are available to you.

The best solution to an unexpected problem is to quell your fear of the unknown by acquiring knowledge of simple survival techniques and survival priorities that give you the basic tools to deal effectively with any emergency situation. This method is so convincing that soon you will experience the growing realization that the things you currently fear losing the most: are actually the ones you really don't need at all.

This knowledge is not new—just mostly forgotten—for, indeed, it is the way all primitive people still live with the earth. They make their own shelters, find, collect and purify their water, build fires with a bow and drill, and hunt and gather their own food—every single day.

If you think about it, it wasn't so long ago that survival and preparedness was a way of life for us, too. Our ancestors, living close to the Earth, knew how precarious their existence was; they took nothing for granted and gave thanks for all they had. We know that the early pioneers depended on the food and supplies that they collected in the summer and fall months and put away to last through the winters. It was a very natural thing to do. It was prudent to be prepared. It assured their survival.

The priorities of **shelter, water, fire and food**—in that order—are the same in any situation, any environment. They are your needs; basic needs that are all provided by our earth in unlimited amounts. Consider that disaster preparedness is a chance to take a simple step to once again touch the earth, respect her and trust in her wisdom.

When you realize and accept that equipped with little more than your brain and your bare hands you can survive any emergency situation, you will accept the challenge of the dark and the unknown. We really are remarkable creatures. We adapt. These instincts are inside you waiting to be let out.

You have to believe and accept that this is really who you are. And that when you are up against it, pushed to your limits in an emergency situation, you too will become a true survivalist.

Not the guns and gold kind, but as Tom Brown, Jr. taught us, *"a true survivalist is a caretaker of the Earth."*

Susan Conniry

Keep it simple— needs not wants

"You'll go a long way toward increasing your mental comfort by realizing that (in a survival situation) you cannot immediately have everything you want, but that you can have everything you need."

Tom Brown Jr., Field Guide to Wilderness Survival

"Grandfather" was an Apache Elder and Medicine Man named Stalking Wolf who taught Tom Brown Jr. how to live with the Earth using wilderness skills. Grandfather travelled the American continent acquiring knowledge of the outdoors wherever he went. He took what he learned, simplified it and tested it in the purity of the wilderness. If it worked, he kept it.

The skills shared in this book are based on those that passed the ultimate test in the wilderness. They are simple and they work.

The information may be used in any emergency situation; from the simplest—a power outage—to the most complex—an earthquake, quarantine situation or evacuation. But, remember the priorities are always the same. And, the more you prepare, the better off you will be. But, in case your supplies run out, or you are away from your supplies, or someone needs them more than you do, remember: knowing what your survival priorities are and how to take care of your needs with little more than your bare hands and your brain will get you through any situation.

Surviving a disaster doesn't require you to be a brain surgeon. In fact, a survival situation is really just a matter of attitude. It is just a change in the day-to-day conditions in which you are accustomed to living. It doesn't have to be frightening. How you perceive it, and how well you deal with it, are really dependent upon how well you are prepared.

A basic understanding of your survival priorities and some simple skills will ensure that you can approach any survival situation with a clear head, whether it is a disaster in the city or you have lost your backpack in the wilderness.

Children excel at these skills. They are flexible to change and besides, no one ever told them they couldn't do it! So, don't worry about them in a survival situation. If you have prepared as a family, it will probably be the kids that do the best!

Shelter

"We do not care about your comfort; we want you to live through the situation."

Believe it or not, this is your number one survival priority!

Though many people are capable of preparing for major breakdowns in power, telecommunications and transportation it is obvious that most of us lack the skills to completely provide for ourselves once a disaster occurs. Yet even those committed to learning the basic survival skills can miss the one element in the equation that is oft times left out—that of self-confidence.

In order to weather a survival/emergency/disaster situation you must first prove to yourself that you can. Every person who is individually prepared takes the pressure off the emergency service agencies. Being unprepared is selfish. It is highly recommended that you take the time to participate in a hands-on survival course. There is nothing better than actually "doing it." Only then will you really understand what will be required of you.

During the last few years of teaching not only wilderness survival but also urban preparedness, it has been amazing to discover that so few people understand the priorities necessary to survive an emergency situation. Recent events make a current evaluation of these priorities even more urgent.

Let me give you some examples. Recently in California, a teenage snowboarder got lost. When he was found several days later, the media coverage demonstrated the lack of understanding that the general public has in regard to survival. The headlines read, "Lost snowboarder lived for six days without food." Somewhere, deep in the third paragraph was the fact that "he died from exposure."

Also recently, an associate of mine asked me to review a manuscript that contained, in part, some advice about emergency preparedness. When I advised him that he had incorrectly assigned water as the number one priority, he replied, "It was my editor's decision." This clearly demonstrates ignorance of the survival priorities.

But, remember, ignorance is no excuse for loss of life. Be prepared.

Learn now.

But first, answer these questions:

- Do you wear clothes?
- Do you live in a building?
- Do you drink liquid?
- Do you heat your home?
- Have you eaten today?

If you answered yes to these questions, then you are a "survivalist" day in and day out; you go about your daily business practicing urban survival skills. You are fulfilling your basic needs and these are the same needs that must be met in an emergency situation.

In any survival situation, natural disaster or man-made emergency the priorities are always the same: shelter, water, fire, and food. Remember that you could survive four days without water and 30 to 40 days without food but without shelter you could die in a matter of minutes—depending on the elements.

 You can live 4 days without water, 30–40 days without food and mere minutes without the right type shelter in an adverse environment.

Shelter, water, fire and food are your needs. All the rest are wants. Knowledge of survival priorities and earth skills can never be taken from you. It is the ultimate insurance.

Shelter

In fact, shelter is your most important survival priority. You always need to be protected from something: the sun, the heat, the wind, the cold, the rain, insects, and injury.

Humans are particularly vulnerable to extreme changes in temperature regardless of whether it's a move towards hot or cold because your body wants to remain in its comfort zone of about 78 °f.

The effects of cold, wind, and rain can lower the body temperature dramatically resulting in a condition known as hypothermia. And once hypothermia of the vital organs sets in, they begin to shut down as they try to conserve heat by drawing in blood from your extremities: head, hands and feet. Add the wind chill factor and any rain to the scenario and very soon you will find yourself in a life-threatening predicament. Remember, hypothermia is by far the most common killer in a survival situation.

Emergency survival shelters

It is prudent and makes sense to be prepared in case of an emergency situation. But what if you don't have your supplies? Maybe you are at work away from your home base, stranded on a highway, or in an airport. Maybe a bear ran off with your pack, or someone needed it more than you. Don't panic. There are simple ways to provide shelter.

The main function of any shelter is to provide warmth, protection and security. A true shelter is one in which your body is the only heat source, in which case, make it small, the smaller the better.

Wilderness shelters

In the wilderness the most effective shelter is a "debris hut." It is built like a squirrel's nest and is small (built to your body size) and well insulated with forest debris, to create dead air space. However, it is far more likely that a natural disaster or emergency situation will occur while you are in an urban setting. In that case, similar to the wilderness debris hut, emergency shelters should be built like a squirrel's nest, well insulated with material.

Urban shelters

As above, these shelters are based on the principal of creating a surrounding cocoon of dead air space that does not require an external heat source. One of the most simple, immediate and effective measures to create dead air space is to simply stuff your clothes. In an urban setting you can use the pages from your phone book, Styrofoam cups, newspaper, plastic bags, or any dry fluffy material.

Without an external heat source all structures such as your home, your office, and your car are nothing more than tents. If there is a power outage, or you run out of fuel for the generator, the inside of the structure quickly becomes the same temperature as the outside air.

In addition to stuffing your clothes you can build a squirrel's nest or a fort. Pick the smallest room that is safe, dry and the least exposed to the cold. Then make a shelter within a shelter. It is best to have a room without windows or with windows facing the sun. Pick a room that is not only convenient but also one with doors that can be opened for ventilation or closed to prevent a draft. Then go hunting!

Gather up all the insulating materials you can find: blankets, pillows mattresses, towels and clothing. Don't forget the drapes and carpeting. The padding under the carpet is excellent too.

Make a carpet burrito • Roll up in a carpet and stuff the inside with pillows and other materials. Don't forget to cover your head.

Make a mattress sandwich • Sandwich yourself between two mattresses with stuffing around the edges—this is an excellent way of sheltering two or more people.

Make a mattress fort • For a larger group of people, this option gives you more room. Make a rectangular box with mattresses as the walls in a corner of the room. Fill the interior with pillows, blankets, and cushions and drape a blanket, quilt or drapes across the entrance. The more insulation you use and the more people huddle together, the warmer it will be.

All these shelters are based on creating dead air space. Anything similar will work. Remember how you made forts when you were a child. That's all there is to it. Build a fort and stuff it with all the insulating material you can find.

Activities

Once your shelter is built, confine your activities to that area. This will conserve energy and cut down on drafts. Shut all doors and windows. Insulate windows by hanging drapes or blankets, but be very conscious and careful about ventilation. And, never bring flames or any combustibles of any kind into the shelter. All cooking must be done a safe distance away from the shelter, whether you are inside or outside.

In your car

If your car breaks down, rip the stuffing out of your seats (remember it is an emergency!) and stuff your clothes. You can stuff the car itself with plant material, trash, anything you can find.

Using your car's heater on a limited basis, run the engine long enough to heat yourself up then turn the car off. Note: always provide ventilation.

You probably keep some emergency equipment in you car, maybe a first aid kit or snow shovelling equipment. Make sure you supplement this with the basics needed to keep warm, to feed yourself, to gather water and to make fire. See the car pack list at the back of this book to ensure you are in a good position to cope wherever you are stranded.

Always make sure you have your cell phone and a phone card or cash available in your car. If the phone networks aren't destroyed or overloaded you will need to contact either the emergency services or your family and business.

In the event of mechanical failure, you should stay with your car. It's a bigger object than you are and easier to find.

If you are buried in the snow, although snow is a great insulator, it will seal out the air. Therefore, be sure to provide yourself a vent hole to the outside world. Also, do not start the engine as the carbon monoxide will build up—it will have nowhere to go. Mark the location of the car for your rescuers to find you.

Clothing

In the shelter war, clothing is your first line of defense against the elements. Clothing creates dead air space around your body. Too much dead air space and you become hot. Too little and you get cold. Therefore, the layering system is recommended for cold weather conditions. This way you can regulate your body temperature by adding or removing layers as you exercise or become sedentary. What you really want to avoid is sweating inside your own clothing. The clothing absorbs the moisture and as soon as you stop moving it evaporates and cools

> **Survival tip C**
>
> Save a life with plastic film
>
> Remove your clothing, take a plastic bag or Saran Wrap, cover your skin with the plastic (direct skin contact) then put your insulating clothes back on. The plastic film will raise your body temperature by at least 20°f and there is no condensation. You don't sweat in it. If you don't believe it, try wrapping up one foot and see the difference.

your skin and you become cold. If you sweat in your clothes, change them! And avoid producing sweat by removing layers as you increase your movement.

The two best fabrics

Fleece • A synthetic material made of plastic. It is made up of millions of tiny air spaces that do not absorb water. It is lightweight, durable and dries quickly. Its disadvantage is that it is bulky, burns and is not wind resistant.

Wool • Natural material made up of hollow hairs. Each hair is a dead air space. Wool contains lanolin, which is natural grease that coats each hair, so protecting it from water absorption. The rule with wool is wet wool is warmer than dry cotton. It is durable material and it doesn't burn. Its only real disadvantage is that when it gets wet it is heavy and takes a long time to dry.

Clothing to include in your personal wardrobe

Watch cap • a hat made of wool or fleece. Did you know that one third of your body heat is lost through your head?

Balaclava • a full-length watch cap made of wool or fleece that completely covers your neck and head.

Scarf • wool or fleece.

Long underwear • top and bottom—wool or fleece—lightweight to expedition weight is available.

Long pants with cargo pockets • wool or fleece—loose fitting so you can bend and move.

Socks • wool or fleece—some people prefer a layer of fleece or light cotton or silk next to their skin and then a wool heavy sock.

Mittens • wool or fleece—long cuff to cover the wrists—some people wear a glove inside their mitten.

Boots • Remember, tight at the ankles, loose at the toes. You need to be able to wiggle your toes with all your socks on. If your feet are cold, loosen your laces. Boots can be made from any material. Be aware that synthetics i.e. plastic, doesn't breathe and creates condensation through your sweat.

Outerwear • You need a high quality coated nylon or pvc rain suit. It should be two-piece, loose fitting, with attached hood. Rain suits made of plastic are 100% waterproof and windproof. Gore-Tex is fine but it is expensive and it doesn't work any better than pvc.

Additionally, consider a broad brimmed fur felt hat. This will protect your head from the rain and keep your head warm. Attach a chinstrap so you don't lose it in a strong wind.

Clothing for extreme heat

In extremely hot temperatures you must limit your physical activities.

Cotton kills! Ask any backpacker. Once wet, it holds the moisture and you will get cold.

Wear light colored clothing that is loose fitting and made of material that can absorb and hold moisture. You want the evaporative effect when you are hot. You'll want a broad brimmed hat and eye protection. In essence, protect your entire body from direct and reflective sunlight.

Survival tip C

Spray clothes with insect repellent, place clothes in a plastic bag, seal the bag for seven days. When removed, this set of clothing will repel gnats, mosquitoes and biting flies for several months. Once washed, you will have to repeat the process. Mosquitoes are attracted to carbon dioxide and seem to prefer the color blue!

Fight off the bugs with:

- Close weave nylon netting to cover your head and body
- Insect repellents (Deet is the best insect repellent)
- Smoke–insects don't like smoke
- Wind
- Cold
- Electronic repellent devices
- Vitamin B-12 taken orally

Water

*"**You never miss the water till the well runs dry.**"*

Roland Howard

Water, water everywhere and not a drop to drink

Water is your second survival priority. Water makes up 75% of the human body and needs to be constantly replenished. Once you have fulfilled your needs for shelter, all your efforts should be concentrated on finding, gathering and treating water.

In a survival situation, an emergency or natural disaster, you must consider all water contaminated. In fact, as we discovered while conducting research for this book, our municipal water treatment plants are having serious problems of their own.

You don't want to drink that

Water almost always contains Giardia and Cryptosporidium. Because humans are remarkably adaptive creatures, in small quantities, these do us no harm, unless you have a compromised immune system. However, if the water entering your municipal treatment plant has been heavily contaminated by human or animal waste, additional numbers of these "critters" slip in unnoticed.

Standard sand filtration and chlorine disinfectant will not systematically remove these contaminants. Giardia is becoming more resistant to chlorine disinfectant and Cryptosporidium is already entirely resistant to disinfectant. In fact neither of these can even be isolated in the water. The only way a public supplier knows there is a problem with the drinking water is after the fact!

Amazingly, the authorities only know about an outbreak after people have already contracted Giardiasis and Cryptosporidiosis. The symptoms include diarrhea, stomach cramps and low grade fever. It is only when infected people seek treatment at a health facility that the infections can be identified by performing tests on fecal samples.

Procedures for identifying the public in the event of an outbreak state that if the lab tests reveal that the infected people drank from a municipal plant that facility is notified and the plant must issue a boil water directive. But by then it can be too late.

When outbreaks occurred recently in Sydney, Australia over 3 million residents were affected. In 1993, an outbreak in Milwaukee, Wisconsin left over one hundred residents dead.

Believe it • A drinking water emergency situation already exists.

Be on the safe side

You must consider all water provided by your municipal water plants to be suspect. In fact, in 1995, the Center for Disease Control and EPA issued a directive that announced that anyone with a severely compromised immune system should consider boiling all their drinking water. The directive, which includes AIDS patients, the elderly and many cancer patients, and could affect 10% of the U.S. population or about 26 million people, was sent to all Public Environmental Health offices.

In San Diego, that directive was forwarded to the individual water treatment plants for their information but there was no mandate that it be distributed to their customers. To date, this information has not been made readily available.

Although self-help groups, including the AIDS community are well advised and aware, hospital cancer centers are still unaware of the EPA's directive. And, if they weren't notified in 1995, it seems highly unlikely that they will be advised now.

If you thought your government, at the federal and local levels cared about your health, maybe you will reconsider the trust you place in them.

Bottled water is suspect too!

The quality of all water you drink today, including bottled water, needs to be carefully evaluated. The FDA (Federal Drug Administration), not the EPA (Environmental Protection Agency), regulates bottled water. The standards are not equal across the board and in some cases are non-existent. Do your homework before you drink.

There is no need to wait for a terrorist attack or other emergency situation. Where water is concerned we are already living in a survival situation.

Storing water in case of an emergency

Being prepared for an emergency situation means always having some stored clean water on hand. One gallon per day per person is a minimum. Clean new water storage containers for camping, ranging in size from one to six gallons are convenient and easy to move. These can be found in the camping/outdoor section of most stores.

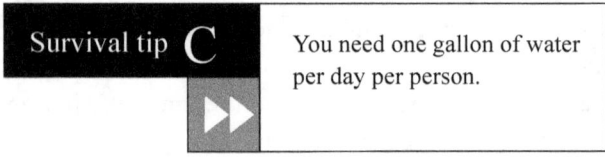

Survival tip ▶▶ You need one gallon of water per day per person.

To store larger quantities of water, the 55 gallon plastic barrels originally used to transport soft drink syrup are excellent. Be careful though, barrels of this kind are also used for storing hazardous chemicals. Make sure you know what was originally stored in these containers before you clean them and store your water.

For convenience and ease of movement, we recommend using recycled Gatorade bottles. They are number one food grade and what you don't use for water are also great for storage of food. You can also use your empty soda bottles, though not as strong, they are quite serviceable. (Don't use milk jugs as they are too flimsy and break.)

Clean thoroughly

Using anti-microbial soap, clean the containers and then air-dry them. Fill with clean water and store the bottles out of direct sunlight. Store your clean water with no additives and then treat it before you use it. (Refer to water treatment section.)

Storing enough water for a few days is simple. However, to store enough water for a family of four for one year you would need 5,110 gallons. Remember that water takes up considerable space and is extremely heavy.

Where do I find drinkable water?

Rainwater

Rainwater is perfectly drinkable water as it falls from the sky. Gather it in clean containers before it touches any other surface. After it touches the ground or dirty surface, it must be considered contaminated and you will need to go through the treatment process.

The morning dew

The morning dew is the simplest method to get perfectly drinkable water but you have to be cautious where you gather it. The safest method is to gather dew from your lawn using a rag, a sponge or some other absorbent material and wring it into a clean container. On a heavily dew-filled morning you can collect about ten gallons of water an hour. This water is perfectly safe, and is drinkable the way it is, However, if there is any question of contamination from any source, e.g. animal excreta, or chemical residues from petrol or pesticides then you should go through the treatment process.

A plastic bag

Place a plastic bag (with no holes) around the branch of a non-poisonous plant and tie it securely to the branch with wire or string. The plant produces water vapour which it releases into the atmosphere. This moisture will condense on the inside of the bag. After a while a sufficient amount of water will gather in the corner of the bag. Remove the bag or cut a small hole in the lowest corner and sip the condensed water.

Beavertail cactus - Opuntia ficus-indica

The beavertail cactus is considered to be edible water. The gray-green, jointed stems are wide and flat resembling the tail of a beaver.

Oval in shape, the stems are 1 to 6 inches wide and 2 to 13 inches long. The stems grow in clumps with flowers from the top edge of the joints. Flowers are followed by a purplish oval fruit more than an inch long with many seeds.

Remember, if it looks parched and withered it probably is. Choose a robust plant. Singe off the spines in an open flame. Slice off the outer skin of the plant and eat the pulp.

Fruit and vegetables

These are full of water. When you eat these you are rehydrating your body as well as nourishing it.

Where else can I find water?

Water does one thing constantly—it flows downhill! All you need to do is find out where it collects.

Clues from the landscape

Trees, such as sycamore, cottonwood and willow are usually good indicators of water as they need a great deal themselves and have extensive root structures to suck water from the ground. If you see cattails - Typha Latifoloa spp - you can be pretty sure water will be under them as they thrive in swampy ground.

All animal trails lead to water. Follow them downhill by looking for animals' footprints, spoor, broken grasses or twigs. Watch where insects and birds are flying, they need water too. Follow the sounds of frogs that live in creek beds and small ponds. Look around for natural depressions and ravines.

In a creek bed, even if no running water is visible, damp sand or mud indicates that there is water present. Dig down and wait for the water to fill the hole. Water can often be found below the surface under large boulders even though the ground may appear dry.

Caution

In the outside environment you are better off dealing with running moving water than you are with anything that is stagnant, that has pooled, or just doesn't look healthy. Be cautious of water from a lake. By the time the water has collected in the lake, it may have collected a host of pollutants and contaminants along the way. It is a much better idea to find the feeder stream entering the lake. A running stream is a great source of water but it must still be considered contaminated. It is important before you gather any water, to look around and determine if the plants and animals nearby are healthy.

Snow, ice, and heavily polluted areas

Though freshly fallen snow may be drinkable without treatment you should always warm and melt it before letting it enter your system. Be aware that bacteria are very commonly found in old snow and ice so always treat it before drinking. Do not collect water from caves, mines, agricultural areas, railroads, roadsides, timber farms and any other areas that may be heavily polluted with herbicides, insecticides and other chemicals.

Survival tip — Before you gather any water look around and check if the plants and animals nearby are healthy.

What about ocean water?

Drinking ocean water without treatment will dehydrate you and ultimately kill you. However, salt water can be used. If you live in an area where ocean floods are common, and can seriously threaten your water supply, keeping a desalination kit as a part of your emergency survival kit may be a sensible precaution. For the person caught unawares in an ocean front catastrophe remember that a solar still will produce clean, drinkable water from ocean water. See the Solar still section below for further details.

What if there's no rain, snow or plants?

So here you are, you're outside, it's not raining or snowing, you have no morning dew, and there are no plants but you have found some water that has pooled on the ground, let's say a mud puddle. This is the water that you are going to treat to get it to the drinkable stage. The analogy that we like to use is that you are panning for gold.

First, remove the big stuff, the sticks, the leaves, and the bugs. You begin by pre-filtering the water through a coffee filter, a T-shirt, sand or a clump of dried grass. This will get rid of the big chunks. Alternatively you can let the water stand for a period of time and the large chunks will settle to the bottom of the container. From there you are going to treat the water all the way to the microscopic level because unless you remove the bacteria, protozoa and the viruses, you may become ill.

Treating water

Now that you have filtered and/or removed the debris from your water it is time to kill the microscopic organisms.

There are three ways to treat the water
- Man-made mechanical devices.
- Chemicals.
- Boiling.

Man-made mechanical devices

There are two types of mechanical hand-held devices: water filters and water purifiers. Water is introduced into either device through a pumping action, is filtered and/or purified and discharged out as drinkable water.

A water filter will remove 99% of all bacterial contamination but it will not remove viruses. In order to remove viruses, you would need to chemically treat the water or boil it.

Water purifiers contain a filter device, a charcoal medium that removes odors and tastes as well as a chemical that will kill viruses.

Survival tip

Filters last longer than purifiers. A good filter will last for about 15,000 gallons of water before you have to replace the inside cartridge. A water purifier will only treat about a 100 gallons of water before the filter cartridge needs to be replaced. All mechanical filters are fragile, and must be maintained, taken apart and cleaned. They are expensive and, obviously, in order to be of use, you must have it with you. This may not always be the case, particularly if your filter is at home and the emergency situation occurs while you are in the office.

Chemicals

Chemicals kill most of the viruses, bacteria and protozoa in contaminated water by essentially poisoning them. This is the method that large municipal water treatment facilities use because it is the most cost effective method of treating large quantities of water.

There are several chemicals available to the individual that can be used for this purpose. These include: pool chlorine, chlorine bleach, and iodine.

Chlorine • Liquid pool chlorine is extremely caustic and must be handled with care. Prior to drinking and in order to make it taste better, water treated with chlorine can be exposed to the air.

Bleach/chlorine bleach • These are also caustic chemicals that must be handled with care. These are regular household bleaches sold in the supermarket. Again, to make it taste better, before drinking, you can expose the water to the air and let the bleach dissipate.

How much bleach should you use? • The rule of thumb for treating a gallon of water is 12 drops and wait thirty minutes. This should kill off the majority of the harmful critters and it is an easy rule to remember.

Iodine • It is a periodic element. It doesn't breakdown into any smaller units. It comes in three forms: as tablets, liquid or as iodine crystals.

Iodine tablets • Convenient but expensive to use. A bottle of tablets may contain 50 tablets. It takes 3 tablets per quart and they retail for $6–8 per bottle. Once opened and not used, they will have a shelf life of several months at which point the iodine has evaporated. We don't recommend tablets unless it is the only thing available.

Liquid iodine • Is usually sold as a liquid solution. Brand names include Provine and Betadine, which are used in the medical and veterinary professions. The least expensive way to purchase it without a prescription is to go to the feed and tack store and buy it in quarts or pints. Use 12 drops per gallon and wait 30 minutes.

Iodine crystals • Small metallic looking beads that when immersed in water, saturate the water to a solution of iodine. The strength of the solution is contingent upon the amount of water and the amount of crystals present. It is variable. Iodine crystals have the advantage of being an almost perpetual iodine making machine.

A small bottle will generally treat about 500 gallons of water before the crystals are used up. This is a very economical method and the one we recommend. For the amount to use, follow the directions on the bottle. (See the manufacturers list in the Resources section at the back of this book for further details.)

Note B ▶▶ Chemicals are caustic and particularly dangerous if mishandled. Use your sense. Don't leave any chemicals where there is a risk of cross-contamination. Keep away from children, food preparation areas, cooking utensils and pets. Some people have an allergic reaction to iodine. Check for this before an emergency situation arises.

Boil it—it's best

After speaking to representatives from EPA, CDC and local municipalities, we decided to keep it simple. The best method of treating water is to boil it.

But for how long? Research provided interesting and varying answers which ranged from just bringing it to a boil, to boiling for 1 minute; to 3–5 minutes; to 10 minutes; to 15 minutes; to 20 minutes. The differing time ranges are based on the contamination level, the source of the water, and the elevation. We did some follow-up research with biologists from Environmental Health offices and determined that the safest method would be to bring the water to a rolling boil and continue boiling from 10–15 minutes depending on your own personal level of paranoia. But, definitely no less than 10 minutes. To minimise the amount lost to evaporation keep the pot covered during the boiling process.

Ten minutes will kill the majority of micro-organisms. However, it may take up to 20 minutes to kill the most resistant of spore-stage viruses. Fortunately, viruses constitute a small percentage of water-borne pollutants but if you have immune-compromised people dependent on this water, such as the young, the old, or particularly weak people you probably should opt for greater caution.

What do you boil the water in?

With a metal container the job of boiling is easy. Fill it with water and put fire under it. As mentioned above, cover it, if possible to reduce evaporation loss.

But, what if you have no metal container?

Boil water in a plastic bag?

Believe it or not you can boil water in plastic sheeting, dry cleaning bags, naugahyde, leather, a pvc raincoat or any other impervious membrane. Sounds impossible? Well it is amazing but it's certainly possible. The idea is to create a "bowl" to hold the water you want to boil.

First, create a dish; second, line the dish with the impermeable membrane. The dish shape can be as simple as a hole in the ground. Conversely, you can build up a mound of sand or gravel with a depression in the middle (volcano shaped). See diagram. The cavity of a tire also works well.

To boil the water you have to bring the fire to the water. One way to do this is to heat stones, concrete or iron weights in a fire and transfer the heated material to the dish. (This wouldn't be a good time to burn your hand so take great care transfering the heated objects.) To prevent the heated object from burning through the plastic, place small

Create a bowl or dish

To boil the water: place concrete, iron weights etc., into a fire, heat up and place the hot chunks into the water.

Put small stones on plastic so that hot rock rests on small stones and not directly on a plastic sheet.

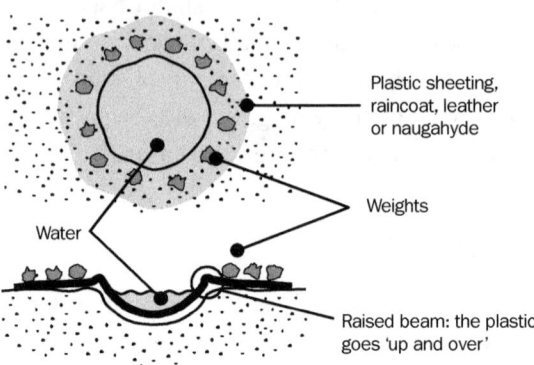

Volcano

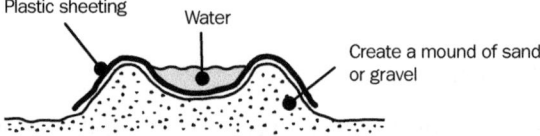

stones to act as a barrier between the membrane and the hot object.

Depending upon the quantity of water in the bowl (a teacup to many gallons) adjust the number and size of stones to accomplish the task. To boil five gallons of water it takes approximately six to eight softball size stones. Once it is boiling, a single stone will keep it boiling from ten to fifteen minutes.

Let the water cool before you drink it, making sure that it is kept in a clean container and kept covered.

Remember the golden rule

There is a rule that goes with collecting stones to use to boil water: never use damp stones. Do not gather your stones from a river bottom or a damp area. These stones can contain moisture that when heated will produce steam, expanding the rock often explosively and with lethal force. Also, Obsidian and Quartz stones are not recommended.

Solar still

A solar still is a man-made device that creates and treats water simultaneously. Its scientific principle is straightforward and involves using a sheet of transparent plastic and the sun to cause water to evaporate and re-condense as liquid. Water that has gone through this condensation/distilling cycle is pure h_2o.

Hole-in-the-ground version

Use a 6'× 6' piece of transparent plastic. Dig a hole that is about knee deep on a adult and as big around. Place a catch basin to collect the water in the dead centre of the hole. Place the plastic over the hole and push the center down into the hole creating an inward cone that points directly over the catch basin (tin can, cup, glass jar, etc.). Seal the edges of the plastic against the ground with stones or any objects to hand.

How it works

The rays of the sun shine through the plastic sheeting. This heats the earth underneath causing any water present in the earth to evaporate as a gas. This gas, or water vapour, rises up and hits the plastic sheeting where it cools, re- condenses and reforms as water droplets. Gravity forces these droplets to flow downhill to the point of the inverted cone where they slide off and land in the catch basin.

In order for a solar still to function there must be water present. This water can be in the soil originally or else it can be added to the solar still. A river bottom in full sunlight with damp sand makes an ideal location. With these parameters present a solar still will produce up to a gallon of drinkable water per day.

If the soil is dry, for instance, in a desert, with no water in the hole, a solar still will produce no water at all. If it is a dry location, you can pour bacterially contaminated water such as pond water or even urine, directly into the dirt, install the solar still and it will produce clean drinking water. You have in effect "seeded" the hole.

You can also seed it with green plant material. Caution must be used that only non-poisonous plants are used as the plants are heated they give up their moisture, which condenses on the plastic and comes back down as water.

Solar still
The five gallon bucket version

Do put in salt or sea water.
Do put in mud or damp sand.
Do put in plant material.

Caution: use only non-poisonous plants; don't use chemically contaminated water i.e. no oil, gasoline, pesticides etc.

Once you've constructed your solar still, remember to place it in direct sunlight.

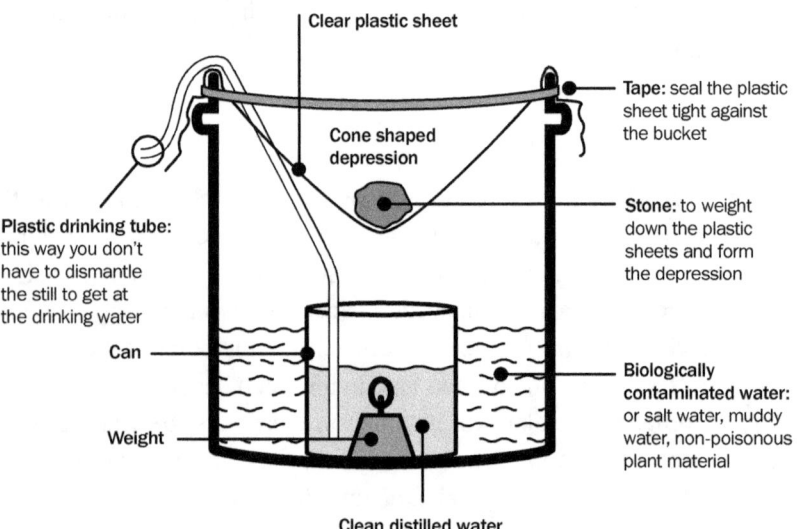

Survival tip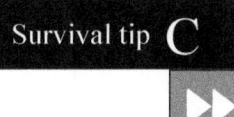

A solar still works well at the beach. In fact, your still will make about twenty gallons of water a day. Perfect for the castaway who remembered to pack a sheet of plastic.

Solar Disinfection, known as SODIS

Developed at the Swiss Federal Institute for Environmental Science and Technology, this technique uses clear plastic bottles filled with water and left in the sun. The heat warms the water and a combination of warm water and utraviolet radiation kills most microorganisms. According to the Institute: "The Solar Water Disinfection (SODIS) process is a simple technology used to improve the microbiological quality of drinking water. SODIS uses solar radiation to destroy pathogenic microorganisms which cause water borne diseases. " Directions for use: 1. Wash the bottle well. 2. Fill the bottle and close the lid. 3. Place the bottle(s) on a corrugated metal sheet. 4. Or put them on the roof. 5. Expose the bottle(s) to the sun from morning till night for at least six hours. 6. The water is now ready for consumption.

Detailed information on SODIS can be found at:

www.sodis.ch/

If you have a limited supply of water there are several things to be aware of...

- Don't eat because it takes water to digest food.
- Don't smoke because it dehydrates your lung lining.
- Don't drink alcohol of any kind because your body has to digest the carbohydrates and the body needs water for the digestion process.
- If you must travel do so only in the cool hours of the evening and the morning.
- Wear light colored clothing, avoiding sun on your skin.
- Move slowly so you don't lose moisture through perspiration or respiration.
- Don't do any physical labor.
- Stay out of the sun and the wind.
- Don't drink your urine. It will dehydrate you even more. (You can, however, use your urine in the solar still.)

Remember you are the best container!

When you do have water, store it inside you not inside a canteen. Conserve the water in your body. There have been horror stories of people who have died with full canteens as a result of trying to conserve their water supply.

Fire

"Humans are the only creatures who use fire as a tool."

Man is the only animal capable of making fire

But, before you slap yourself on the back and wallow in your superiority over the animals, bear in mind that fire has been responsible for making us creatures of comfort and addicts of convenience. We love fire. We are fully dependent on fire. We need fire.

With fire you have heat, you can purify your water and cook your food. But fire also warms the human heart and goes a long way to making you feel more secure. Think of the times you have sat around a campfire and experienced that sense of comfort. Most of all it pushes back the dark—one of our greatest fears.

And yet, fire is too often taken for granted. It is hard to believe that fire is considered by all primitive people to be a sacred skill when in our modern society it is as simple as turning on a light switch, adjusting the thermostat, cooking on a "Jenn-Air" stove top, striking a match or flipping a "Bic."

We cannot, with words alone, express the magical transformation that occurs when you create a "coal" using the primitive bow and drill or hand-drill method. Neither can we establish in you the appreciation of how important fire is in our daily lives. We can, however, tell you that when man-made power goes out and you are without fire for even a few days, it will become precious beyond words.

In scientific terms, fire is nothing more than friction. It is the energy of the sun. Yet by using primitive techniques to make fire in a wilderness setting it becomes an art. The tools you use must be properly carved. Time, patience and skill produce a coal that is laid gently into a bird nest of tinder. Cradling it gently like a baby, you nurture it and breath life into it. As the tinder bursts into flames, you place it into the kindling designed like a tipi within the properly located fire pit. It is a moment unlike any other when you take the purely physical act of rubbing two sticks together and bring forth, once again, the energy of the sun.

Many of the students at our wilderness school relate that it is an incredibly spiritual moment being at once overwhelmed and immensely grateful for the gift. In fact, the ability to make fire using primitive skills gives you a sense of freedom. You feel invincible, for you can go anywhere and make fire!

Starting a fire

Lighters • These provide thousands of lights and they even continue to work after prolonged washing in the pocket of your jeans, they are seemingly indestructible! (A tip for those who do keep a lighter in their pocket—wrap a rubber band around the lighter, it will prevent it from falling out when you sit down).

Magnesium fire blocks • Purchase them at any drug store that has a camping section. A magnesium fire block is a large chunk of magnesium with a flint like material running down one side. You scrape off the magnesium with a file or knife creating a pile about the size of a dime. Using the steel from your knife or file you create a spark by scraping it against the flintside of the magnesium fire block. Scrape the sparks onto the magnesium shavings. It instantly ignites, burning at 5,400°f. Using just the flint (spark side of the fireblock) you can ignite dry material such as cotton balls, 00 steel wool, or cattail down. This way you save your magnesium for when you have to light damp material. Magnesium fire blocks can be purchased from sporting goods stores.

Batteries • An effective method for starting fire is by using batteries: Take a 9-volt transistor radio or smoke detector battery—the flat square ones—and touch both terminals to a fluffed up mass of 00 steel wool. It will ignite instantly. Another option is to short circuit any size battery by using a piece of fine wire from lamp cord or phone wire. Cut a length of wire about 6–8 inches. Touch one end of the wire to one end of the battery; run the body of the wire through combustible material, paper, steel wool, cotton and touch the other end to the other end of the battery. This will cause the wire to heat to the melting point and ignite the combustible material. The smaller size batteries take longer to heat the wire.

Chemicals • There are various chemical ways to start fire which are available on the market. Fire is created when two separate chemicals are combined together and ignite into open flame. Be careful, they are dangerous.

Glass • Another option is a magnifying glass, or a spectacle lens, which of course must be done on a sunny day! The magnifying glass or lens will concentrate the sunlight down to a fine point creating enough heat to ignite paper, cotton, dry grass, etc.

Safety Note G

Be sure to insulate your hands when using batteries because the wire gets hot and will burn you! Stay away from large batteries like your car battery. Too much kick! These can explode as can any battery but a car battery has far too much energy and the potential for problems is too great.

> **Note** A word of caution, do not use accelerants like gasoline or kerosene if you can't get a fire going by normal means. For example, do not use gasoline to try to get wet wood burning. Don't turn an emergency situation into a dire situation.

Practice beforehand

If you need to make a fire in an emergency you should be confident of your abilities. Frustration can lead to mistakes. It is always a good idea to practice making fire by going camping or having a barbecue. Start from the smallest material and add to it, building to the larger pieces. Also remember it takes wood to burn wood. Consider all wood found on the ground as being wet. Though you must first have a way to light them, candles are an excellent way to get wet wood burning.

If you know you will need to make fires over the course of a few days, for instance if you are on the move, or if you have to let your fire die away during the day, it is a sensible precaution to dry, fine kindling out by your fire and then keep it dry in a waterproof bag or pocket. This will save you time the next time you have to make a fire.

Always prepare your fire pit with a "tipi" or pyramid shaped mass of kindling before you attempt to start your fire. You should **never** make a fire inside your shelter. You are already in an emergency situation;

don't make it worse by burning your shelter down or asphyxiating yourself. Any open flame consumes oxygen and produces poisonous carbon monoxide gas. In addition there is the physical danger of lighting something on fire. When you do have an open flame of any kind whether it is a candle or a campfire, have a designated person be on "fire watch." Their sole function is to keep tabs on the fire.

Lamps without batteries

In an emergency, when it gets dark—go to bed. Save your resources until sun up. However, if there is an injured person you may need light. If you need to have fire for light, create a lamp.

Jar lamp

′ A clean jar filled with cooking oil.

′ T-shirt hem or towel hem as a wick.

Directions

Punch a hole through the lid using a Phillips head screwdriver. Punch the hole from the inside to the outside of the lid. Push the wick through, screw the lid on and light the wick. Adjust wick as necessary.

Jar lamp

Potato lamp

This is easy. Just stand a potato on its end and cut the bottom off so it stands flat. Cut the top end off and put to one side. Take a spoon and scoop out the inside creating a reservoir. Pierce a thickish hole through the top section you cut off. Fill the reservoir with any type of cooking oil. Create a wick using the hem of a T-shirt. Soak the wick in the oil. Push the wick up through the hole in the top piece of potato so that one end sticks up above. Replace the potato "lid" back on top of the reservoir so the other end of the T-shirt hem is sitting in the reservoir. Light the piece sticking out and hey presto! By adjusting the wick from time to time this lamp will burn for as long as there is oil in the reservoir.

Spiral chip lamp

Take a shallow pan and fill it with sand or rice or dirt, or some other non-flammable material and place chips upright, overlapping edge to edge. Tortilla chips work best. Start on the outer rim and spiral the chips inward, each chip standing up and barely touching the one next to it. Light the first chip. As it burns, it will light its neighbor and so on, slowly working its way, chip by chip, around the pan and around the spiral.

Cotton balls

Set cotton balls with Crisco or Vaseline mushed into them on a non-burnable surface and ignite them. They will burn for about eight minutes.

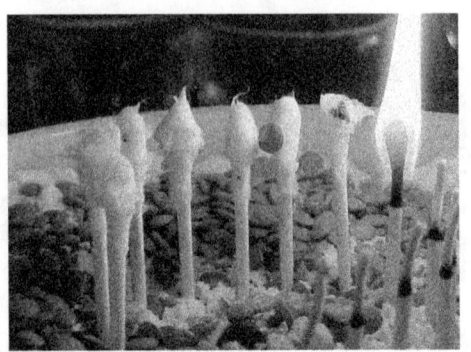

Q-Tip lamp

′ Q-Tips.

′ Lard.

′ Bowl.

′ Sand, rice, flour.

Dip the ends in lard. Stick them in an appropriate medium, i.e. rice, sand, flour in a bowl. Space each Q-Tip about one pencil width apart, more or less. Spiral them around the bowl. Light the first one and voila!

Don't forget that you can use multiple light sources. For example, more than one cotton ball, more than one potato lamp.

For warmth

When it is not possible to sit or sleep near the fire you may need a way of keeping yourself, a child or an injured person warm. If you are sleeping in a shelter remember you must never take a naked flame into it. These methods allow you to take warmth to the person who can't come to the fire.

> **Safety Note G**
>
> Remember never to collect your stones from a river bottom or an area where they are exposed to long-term dampness. The water seeps into the center of the stone over time and if placed in a fire and heated, that water turns to steam and it expands and may explode with lethal intensity.

Hot sand bags–or socks...

Heat sand in a metal frying pan over your fire. Put the hot sand into a sock or water bottle and use this as you would a heating pad or hot water bottle. Remember not to leave hot objects alongside people who are unable to move themselves, or the object, away from them as continued application of a hot object may cause burning to occur.

Hot rocks

You can heat iron weights from your bench set, concrete chunks, or dry stones in the centre of your fire. Take these heated items (use tongs) and place them on a non-burnable surface. These provide radiant heat. They give off no carbon monoxide gas and consume no oxygen. Treated with care so as not to contact any flammable surface, these can be used in an enclosed space.

Candle and blanket

This one requires extreme caution and should only be used when all other options are unavailable. Take a hot stone or a small candle. Place it inside a metal can. Set the metal can between your legs and wrap a blanket around you forming a tent-like structure. It is not recommended for children, the sick or the elderly and should not be attempted under your shelter.

Urban fire

Generators are dangerous. They are complex and unless you really know what you are doing with them you are better off using simpler forms of heat and light providers. Every year someone dies because they pulled a generator into the house, turned it on, went to sleep and never woke up. In addition, it is foolish and irresponsible to store quantities of fuel anywhere, particularly in "fire" country. If you have a fireplace with a proper chimney and adequate ventilation you should keep logs, firestarters and matches where they can be found easily in an emergency.

If you are in an apartment building with no fireplace and no obvious means of heat you should have some contingency plans. You can stay warm by building a shelter. You should have food stored and some water. Your fire needs may be minimal. However, if you decide to use a stove or light candles, remember, any naked flame is a danger, especially in such a building while the emergency services are otherwise occupied.

Never leave any flame unattended and keep a fire extinguisher or fire blanket handy. A wet blanket would serve if nothing else is available. Remember that a fire can be stopped by depriving it of oxygen so a fire blanket will suffocate a small fire in its early stages. Never throw water on a fat fire, the droplets will carry the flames across the room and start more fires. And make sure there is enough air, adequate ventilation is a must because carbon dioxide, a product of combustion, is a killer in an enclosed space.

It is a sensible precaution to keep a small camping gas burner, along with spare gas canisters in your apartment so that at the very least you can sterilize water, boil water for drinks or hot water bottles, and prepare basic hot food. These come in a variety of sizes from Walmart. Buy the one you can store most easily.

Although a survival situation, in a sense, seems no more than winning a struggle against the environment with the main goal of getting back to the comfort and convenience of civilization, it is more than that. As our umbilical cord with society is severed, we all have to learn to live again as primitive people—using our own energy to provide our needs. It is experiencing the direct reward system—energy in—energy out. You use your skill and energy to make fire, which will provide you with heat, light and ways to purify your water and cook your food. It is simple, if you make fire—you eat! Even in a modern setting, you can duplicate the sacredness of fire. All it takes is a humble attitude. But remember, fire is never a given. Be appreciative, accept the gift and be grateful.

Food

"As long as we have money, food seems ours for the taking."

Tom Brown Jr. | City and Suburban Survival

"Thanks for the grub"

It isn't fancy but we share this humble prayer before each meal. Not only are we grateful in a reverent sense but also for reasons of practicality.

Food is your last survival need. For adults in good shape, true starvation doesn't begin until about 40 days without food. Your first few days without food bring about grumpiness and a shrinking of the stomach. This is merely your attitude. You are not going to starve to death. However, food provides comfort, energy, and helps relieve stress in an emergency situation.

"Thanks for the grub"

So although food is the last in the "sacred" order of survival priorities it is really the lynchpin in any urban emergency situation (natural or man-made disaster). Anyone can make shelter. With a cigarette lighter, anyone can have fire. With a filter or chemicals, water can be purified. But, without food an emergency situation quickly becomes a bleak and debilitating experience. In an emergency you need more energy to deal with everything.

A New York City dweller once sarcastically asked if I am suggesting that 30 million people hunt and capture rabbits in Central Park. I am not. Though hunting and trapping animals is part of the training in our Wilderness Challenge courses, and would prove useful in the suburbs or open countryside, these techniques would hardly suffice in an urban environment. The best choice for city dwellers (and everyone else for that matter) is stored long-term food.

Food storage planning

So, since we are such lousy hunters and farmers, the most prudent plan of action is to invest some time and energy into a food storage program. In an emergency situation, you are going to be under great stress and using a tremendous amount of calories, more than you would usually expend due to stress, injury, anxiety and having to do everything yourself. So start to plan now.

Select what kinds of food and how much food you need to store for you and your family. Calculate the caloric needs of your group. Normally, children, teens and men need around 2,200 calories per day; women need around 1,400—2,000, elderly women around 1,400 and elderly men around 1,800. In an emergency situation, especially if it is cold or people are moving around more than usual they will require more food to be comfortable.

Remember that preparation is the key to survival. The simplest thing you can do so you don't have to relocate against your wishes, either planned or unplanned will revolve around your food storage program.

Food storage containers

An excellent storage container is an empty wide-mouthed juice bottle of the type that Gatorade and virtually all the juices come in. They range in sizes from half pints to one gallon. Using a bottlebrush and anti-microbial soap, clean the containers and the lids, then air dry. Containers can be filled with all of your stored foods, including lard that can be melted, poured in and left to reset.

Where to store the bottles?

If they are placed in your house they are subject to destruction whether earthquake, fire, flood, theft and also are subject to variants in temperature, light and humidity.

If you have access to land, an effective place to store your bottles is to lay out an area for burial in the ground. Before burying the bottles however, secure the cap by covering it with Henry's 208 Wet Dri Roofing Cement. Let it dry to a hard consistency. This seals the bottle one hundred percent.

In the area that you have laid out you can dig the holes for each individual bottle using a fence post or posthole digger. Now your bottles and your food are in a temperature-controlled environment, out of the light, safe from fire, and theft. A ten-foot by ten foot ($10' \times 10'$) square could easily hold enough food for a family of four for six months.

If you do not have access to land you may have a cellar or attic or loft space in which you can store some food. Take care that everything is well sealed and rodent-proofed. But you must have an alternative depot for your supplies in case your house is destroyed in the emergency incident. Burying your supplies really is the best alternative and it is worth trying to plan ahead to ensure that whatever happens, you will be self-reliant. This will be difficult in a city and you will have to use your imagination. Bear in mind that people seen burying things late at night in the city are more than likely to end the evening in conversation with a police officer so you may have to be more than usually resourceful!

Tempting as it may be to share the responsibility of storing food with a friend you should ensure that you are completely self-reliant. In the event of a catastrophe your friend may be missing, or their extended family may show up and expect to be fed.

Sourcing food

Some of you will order from a "pre-packaged food" supplier. One advantage to purchasing survival food this way is it requires little energy and effort on your part. You place your order and await delivery. A disadvantage, however, is the cost.

"Doing-it-yourself" is the "preferred" way because it gets you into the habit of learning how you will survive a disaster situation"—by exerting your own energy and effort"—and it gives you an immediate reward. You have your food now.

The following is a preliminary guideline to your survival food needs. The list is not all-inclusive, as many of you may want to include your own personal items.

Emergency food list

These foods have been selected for their long term storability and the fact that they include proteins, quick carbohydrates and sugars. There is an adequate variety and require no refrigeration.
Beans • pintos, lentils, legumes

Cocoa | tea | coffee

Hard candy

Hard red winter wheat

Honey

Lard • beef

Non-fat instant dry milk powder

Popcorn

Powered juice • orange, lemonade

Salt

Seeds • Quinoa, linseed, flax

Soup base • chicken, beef, tomato

Soy sauce

Spices • garlic, onion, pepper, vinegar

Sugar

White rice (brown rice goes rancid)

Whole corn

You will have noticed that lard is included in the list of food supplies. In a survival situation, you will be expending an enormous amount of energy that will need to be replaced. Lard contains the most caloric energy of any known food type at roughly 130 calories per tablespoon, and energy from fat is what your body runs on. Added to other foods such as soup, it gives one the feeling of feeling full.

Lard is the base of pemmican (a mixture of dried meat and lard used by Native Americans). Lard needs no refrigeration and has no expiration date. In addition it can be used as lubricant, candles, trap bait.

Next on our list are the staples, wheat, rice, corn, and beans. Rice, corn and beans eaten together provide a complete protein which means you don't have to find meat, this protein combination doubles for meat and is a great deal easier to catch and keep!

To save fuel for cooking soak your grains in water so they become soft. Many beans such as lentils, peas and mungbeans will sprout when left to soak in water for a day or two. These are particularly nutritious, very high in protein and can be eaten as fresh green vegetables.

Canned foods

Canned foods are an excellent above ground way to plan a varied emergency food diet. They store easily and last anywhere from six months to twenty years. Buy canned food by the case to get the quantity discount. Using a permanent marker date and identify the contents of the cans and use them in sequence (new ones are rotated in as you use the "oldest" cans first.) Don't eat food from dented or "blown" cans.

Be sure to have a non-electric can opener.

Baby foods

Formula, dried foods and bottled foods should be stored, unopened, in their original cans or sealed into plastic containers to protect them from damp, insects and mold. Glass bottles should be sealed with wet/dry roof cement. Sterilising tablets (ask at your drug store) should be kept with your emergency supplies for cleaning infants' feeding items such as bottles and cups as your dishwasher and its germ killing heat may be out of action. Do not bleach rubber teats. If you do not have sterilising liquid or tablets, boil bottles and teats for 10 minutes and leave to cool in the water until use.

Dried fruits and vegetables

You may want to purchase a dehydrator and dry your own fruits and vegetables at home. These can be stored long-term in plastic juice bottles. To store dried vegetables, add salt and to store dried fruit, add sugar. Dried beans can be sprouted in water and eaten as fresh vegetables.

Non-food items

You will also need cooking utensils, cups, plates, bowls, cutlery, hand-operated can opener, pot holders, towels, trash bags, cutting boards, dish soap, bleach, disinfectant and a tub to wash your dishes in. A sharp knife is essential.

A hand grinder to mill the grain is vital if you store whole grains

If you cook on an open fire, one of the best cooking vessels is a wok. The best kind have wooden handles and are made of heavy steel. The bowl-shaped design concentrates the heat and allows it to be used with a minimum amount of fuel and its shape enables it to sit at any angle in an open fire. (Ensure all open fires are made outside.)

Knives

You don't have claws and you aren't efficient with your teeth so you need to invest in good quality knives. We recommend three sizes. You should have all three.

Small knife

A Swiss Army knife or Leatherman tool on a lanyard so you don't lose it. This is for all your fine, delicate work, i.e. trimming your nails, making holes in bones, and so on.

A medium sized workhorse

This knife will do the majority of your work, i.e. carving things by hand, whittling, all middle ground work. Highly recommended is the Buck Vanguard #692 or the Buck Zipper with a rubber handle. It is a nice size and fits both men and women.

Big knife!

This is used for heavy chopping activities. It is the size of a meat cleaver or machete.

Safety Note G

Extreme care must be exercised when using knives. Always make sure you carve away from your body. If you have never used a knife, practice whittling. Keep your knife sharp.

Cooking

Your home may have a fireplace which you use mostly as a cheering decoration. In a power outage or bigger emergency you can cook on it if you use great care. Remember to cook on the glowing hot embers, the heat is easier to control and you run less risk of burning yourself. Use pans without special coatings, they will be easier to clean with steel wool. A wok with a handle makes a very controllable cooking utensil. You may want to place metal bars across the firebasket for the pot to sit on if you are boiling water.

If you have no fireplace but a number of people to feed you could use a system that we use day to day: a Coleman camping stove, get a two burner from Walmart, with a 1—2 gallon cylinder propane tank. This is larger than the regular camping sizes usually bought with these stoves. Walmart also sells the appropriate connections (hose and regulator) to connect the stove to the propane. A 2-gallon tank should last up to two months—using it all the time!

For smaller dwellings, in the car or boat, or for fewer people, a small backpack type camping stove is an excellent way to prepare warming drinks and meals and to supply boiling water for hot water bottles. Make sure that you can pressurize the stove fuel bottle by a manual pump.

Mountain Safety Research makes an excellent, lightweight, reliable, efficient cook stove.

Survival tip

- A number 10 coffee can with a detachable coathanger handle is very handy for boiling water, carrying water, digging holes, you can even bake bread in it.
- A frying pan lid used as a frying pan. Remove the handle, make sure there is no hole and invert it. These are lightweight and very inexpensive.
- Keep books on wild edible plants and fungi native to your area in your emergency food storage kit.

Grow your own

Purchase some non-hybrid seeds and plant your own garden. If you are in an apartment, consider a planter box on the windowsill. Native Seed Search in Tucson Arizona — http://desert.net/seeds/home.htm — has an excellent supply of seeds that can reproduce themselves from one crop to the next.

Survival tip

' When storing grains in your own containers, pour a handful of salt inside before you screw the cap on. The salt will kill any insects present in the grain.

' Seal caps with Henry's 208 Wet Dri Roofing Cement. The container is now waterproof and can even be buried underground.

' Store out of direct sunlight in a safe, temperature-controlled environment or under the ground. (If your residence is demolished by the elements i.e. fire, flood, storm, earthquake, or civil unrest you will still be able to access your emergency food supply).

Man as hunter...

Most of us are lousy farmers but there are even more lousy hunters. It is the one survival skill that we can't replicate readily. In a primitive survival situation the simplest weapon known is a rock. However, most people tend be pretty lousy shots with a rock. The second oldest weapon known is a stick. Picked up and thrown it cuts a wide swath increasing your chances of hitting an object many times.

What do you throw your stick at? In the animal kingdom, the rule to remember is if it's finned, furred, feathered, and scaled—you can eat it.

In addition to the primitive method of a throwing stick, there are other techniques for securing food. One of the simpler methods is to use a snare. A snare is simply a wire or cord noose placed on a trail that animals use, which slips over the head of a creature as it walks down the trail. Wire for a snare can be procured from lamp cords or phone wire. The animal tightens the noose with its weight and chokes to death. The other end of the snare is secured to an immovable object such as a tree or post, or weighed down by a rock.

If you snare an animal it might be alive when you find it. Do not approach and subject yourself to a bite risk. Spear or club the animal at arm's length.

With twenty snares pre-made and placed on various animal runs or trails, or burrow holes in the ground, you should be able to procure from one to five animals per twenty traps. These snares require no bait.

On the other hand, you might want to consider purchasing a ·22 rifle. A simple, cheap, reliable, ·22 long rifle cartridge properly aimed can take down or kill any size game in North America. A reliable ·22 rifle should be a bolt action type made from stainless steel. These are simple, light guns and can easily be held and used by both women and men.

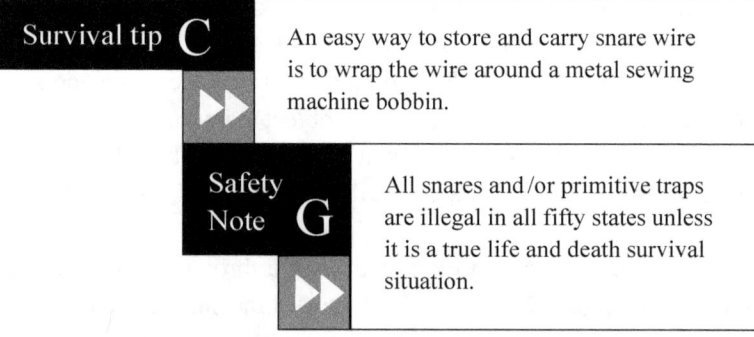

| Survival tip C | An easy way to store and carry snare wire is to wrap the wire around a metal sewing machine bobbin. |

| Safety Note G | All snares and/or primitive traps are illegal in all fifty states unless it is a true life and death survival situation. |

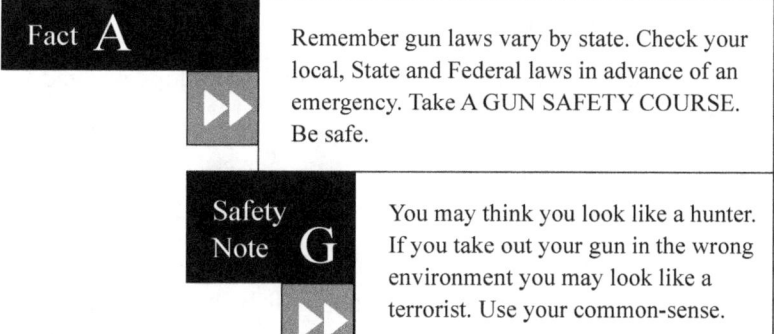

Fact A — Remember gun laws vary by state. Check your local, State and Federal laws in advance of an emergency. Take A GUN SAFETY COURSE. Be safe.

Safety Note G — You may think you look like a hunter. If you take out your gun in the wrong environment you may look like a terrorist. Use your common-sense.

Meat and game preparation

Some of the elements of self-reliance are not easy for those of us who have fully adopted consumerism and with it the pre-packed, film-sealed portions of meat we buy in supermarkets. The real thing will be tough—even reading about it will make you feel nauseous—doing it will be worse. But this is what we are programmed to do. To survive. And if hunting and preparing meat is what it takes, you will find that you can overcome man's recently-acquired reluctance to use nature's bounty. Ethical vegetarians will do well to skip this part and cut to the section dealing with "gathering"!

After you kill an animal immediately bleed it by cutting its throat. If you have to drag it to wash it do so before you skin it. If you can, leave the carcass to cool before cleaning, gutting and skinning as fleas and other parasites will desert a cold body.

Skinning large game

Step 1 • Support body, belly up, preferably on a slope wedged with stones.

Step 2 • Cut out genitals, udder, musk glands (if you know where they are, on a deer they are on the inside thighs near the knees).

Step 3 • Split hide from tail to throat with a shallow cut that doesn't cut through to the stomach. Insert your knife between the hide and the body and start to peel it back a few inches on each side so that the fur doesn't get in the meat when you start to cut.

Step 4 • Split the chest cavity along the sternum. You will need some strength for this but cutting to one side—where the ribs join the bone rather than straight down the middle, is easier.

Step 5 • Put your hand inside and cut the windpipe and gullet as high up and near to the skull as possible. Work your way down the body cavity lifting out internal organs and cutting only where necessary to free them. The entrails—heart, liver and kidneys are all edible although in the unlikely event that you catch a polar bear give its liver a miss. The concentrated levels of Vitamin A would be enough to kill you!

Step 6 • Urine can spoil the meat so be careful cutting away the bladder, pinch the urethra, cut past where you have pinched it and remove and discard the entire bladder.

Step 7 • The anus is removed by cutting around it on the outside of the hide and pulling it back through the body cavity to be discarded.

Step 8 • If you need the hide, peel back the skin cutting the membrane between the hide and the meat. You will have to cut the skin along the hoof, or paw, and peel it backwards over these extremities.

Small game

Make a 2 inch slit horizontally across the back of a squirrel or chip-

> **Survival tip**
> The blood of animals is nutritious and a good source of salt. Boil it. It's a good base for soups.

munk, between the skin and the flesh. Insert your second and third fingers of each hand and pull back the skin over the body, unpeeling it. Remove the innards, more or less as above, with less difficulty.

When handling meat try to wear gloves to avoid pathogens entering the human body through cuts in the skin. These pathogens can include Hepatitis, Rabies, Talaremia, (Rabbit Fever).

All meat should be cooked well because of this potential for infection, especially wild meat. Although it won't be full of antibiotics it could have pathogens, worms, etc. Don't worry, cooked properly it will taste great and thorough cooking until the juices run clear, not bloody, will ensure that all the pathogens are destroyed.

Fishing in an emergency

Leaving aside all the refinements of a modern fisherman we are reduced to fashioning a hook and line, a net or a sharp stick. Fish can be anywhere, ponds, rivers, ornamental gardens, the sea. They can be difficult to catch. We give here some very basic hints on how to catch a fish.

Making a fishhook

You will have to make a fishhook that's the same size for the fish in the area so you may have to experiment if you don't know what you are fishing for. Cut a piece of wood around two inches long and as thick as two matchsticks and cut a notch about ¼" an inch from one end. Lay whatever point you have available: a pin, nail, pointed wood, thorn, piece of bone, etc., in the notch and lash with a secure knot, preferably a clove hitch, several turns to bind it tight and another clove hitch. You need to keep the point well secured to the wood and capable of holding firm against a squirming fish.

Lines

You can make these by twisting strands of any fibres together, the inside of bark, grasses, etc. A better idea is to carry line in your emergency kit along with a set of fishhooks.

Bait

Look around and see what's there. Crustaceans such as small crabs, shrimp, etc can be bait as well as food for you (scoop up with a net or can), there may also be worms and insects or minnows. If you catch or find a fish look at its stomach contents and try to replicate what you find there using shiny metal, colored cloth, feathers etc.

When to fish

Fish generally feed at twilight, that is at dawn or dusk, or just before a storm. Many crabs and lobsters are nocturnal. You may need to net these nippers.

An improvised net

Find a small forked sapling and take off your shirt. Tie the ends of the branch together so that it forms a circular frame, tie the shirt so that the neck and armholes are closed and fold the bottom of the shirt over frame and secure with pins, wire or whatever you have available. Heavy mesh, such as a fruit sack, could also be used.

What not to eat

Some fish are poisonous but these tend to look repellent. They often don't have scales but smooth or rough skin, bristles or spines and dwell in rocky or coral reefs and muddy shores. The toxic substances in their skin cannot be cooked out—so don't try them!

Do not eat fish eggs found in clusters or clumped on rocks or logs.

Shellfish that are uncovered at high tide should not be eaten and remember that mussels are poisonous in tropical areas during the summer.

...and man as gatherer

In the plant kingdom there are tens of thousands of known edible plants. You should familiarize yourself with the ones that are native to your location. But in case you are caught unawares away from home here are six common plants which could feed you in an emergency: acorns, pine trees, cattails, broad blade grasses, yucca and seaweed. There are no known poisonous sea plants.

Acorns

Acorns are edible in any stage of their development and contain more protein that hamburger. They should be collected in the fall so if you are looking in the winter you will be competing with the other animals, bugs and birds! To prepare them for consumption, make sure there are no holes bored in the side, crack the outer shell off to reveal the soft inner nut. Most acorns are inedible due to their tannic acid content. Luckily, tannic acid is water-soluble. Chop the nut into pieces. Place in a pot and cover with water. Bring the water to a boil and boil for twelve minutes. Drain off the liquid. Add water and repeat the boiling process as many times as necessary to remove the bitter taste. Once you have removed the tannic acid, you can eat them the way they are or dry the nut pieces and store or grind into a flour for later use.

Pine trees

All pine trees have pinecones. Find the cones when they are closed. Pick them and place them two feet from a heat source, i.e. a campfire. In fifteen to twenty minutes the pinecone will open up thinking that it is springtime. You simply tap onto a hard surface and collect up the pine nuts. Remove the papery bract by rubbing and or singeing. The hard outer hull surrounding the pine nut is also edible. Pine needles chopped and boiled in water for three minutes will yield a tea that has more Vitamin C than orange juice.

Cattails

All species of cattails are plants that grow in fresh water areas, sometimes brackish areas, but never in salt water. A cattail has some edible part in any season of the year. Probably the simplest thing to do is eat the young tender shoots as they emerge out of the water. In addition the green seed heads can be boiled in water for three to five minutes and eaten like corn on the cob. Cattails provide material for making everything from shelter, to rafts, mats, baskets, clothing and tools. Once all the pollen has been removed from the pollen head, you can use the top shaft as a toothbrush.

Grasses

All broad bladed grasses from your lawn to bamboo are edible. Simply chew the stems, the seeds, the roots, the leaves, swallow the liquid and spit out the roughage—you cannot digest the plant material but you can get the nutrients from swallowing the juice.

Yucca

This versatile plant provides cordage, soap, food, firemaking material, material for various tools such as fishing floats, canteens, arrow quivers, tinder storage. The edible parts are the white flowers, the green seed capsules, the black seeds and the baked main stalk.

Seaweed

Gather it up fresh, make sure any creatures, snails, sand etc. are rinsed off and dry it in the sun on clean grass or hanging in the air.

It can be eaten baked, added to soups or used as a wrap around rice. Seaweed contains about 25% protein plus a percentage of iodine.

Insects

Insects actually comprise a large percentage of the world's food. It's just that we humans usually turn our noses up at them. Insects are about sixty percent protein. The best bet for catching insects is to find them when they are massing, in their hive, or in their dormant stage otherwise it is a waste of your energy. Fry them and then grind them and add the powder to various foods. Soft bodied insects are best.

Eggs

All eggs are edible whether from birds, reptiles, or fish. Cook them all well.

Take It One Day At A Time

A natural disaster often creates a situation similar to a war zone, with power outages, food supplies cut off, communication lines down. But before you lament that there is no way you could live through a disaster of that dimension, consider the stoic Birtish who lived for many years under severe conditions during World War II. Susan's father, Frank, who was a paratrooper during the war, has told us the stories of the devastation of the cities, the ration lines and constant black outs. And, at the end of each story he would tell us that they got through it "one day at a time." To be prepared is necessary, natural and above all, simple.

Sanitation

"Soap and education are not as sudden as a massacre, but they are more deadly in the long run."

Mark Twain

Good sanitation practice though prudent on a daily basis, is vital in an emergency situation

It is your responsibility to minimize any risk of infection and reduce the spread of infectious diseases. Remember to keep washing your hands, keeping yourself clean, keeping your space clean and observing good work habits. Ensure that there is a system in place which allows everyone access to clean water, clean lavatories (however basic) and that the sick and young are kept clean.

To maintain as hygienic an environment as possible you should follow some basic guidelines:

Washing your hands, hair and body

- Rub hands together vigorously for several minutes to help kill germs.
- Use soap, it is naturally anti-bacterial.
- Consider using chlorine cleanser on your hands.
- Have a wash cloth available for a sponge bath.
- Keep hair lice-free by preventative combing with a fine-toothed lice comb, which is available from any drug store. Combing strips eggs from hair and breaks the legs of any developed lice, which prevents them from mating. Lice shampoos contain strong chemicals, including organo-phosphates which can cause serious allergic reactions in some people. With lice, as with germs, prevention is way better than the cure.
- Keep fingernails and toenails clean and trimmed.
- Shave hair and beard short if long-term.

Doing the dishes

Your dishwasher may not be working. Think back to the Girl Scouts way for washing dishes!

- Use hot, soapy water to cut grease and to sanitize.
- Rinse in clean water.
- Dip in diluted bleach solution to sanitize.
- Air dry, in the sun if possible.

Household hints

If you have had the foresight to stock up for an emergency you will have ensured you have an adequate supply of disposable diapers, toilet paper, feminine hygiene items, bleach and cleaning supplies but you may have to make do with what you have available at home.

- You can wash your clothes in a bucket or the tub and dry them in the sun and wind by erecting a clothesline. This is as simple as a rope stretched from two poles or tied between two fixed points. If you have no clothes pins, double the rope/twine on itself and twist it slightly before fixing it. Poke the ends of the clothes between the twists to hold them in place if there is a strong wind. Clothes will also dry well on bushes.
- Floss and brush your teeth regularly—if you run out of toothpaste you can use charcoal (burned wood from your fire) or baking soda.
- Use paper plates, cups and towels, not plastic. You can burn the waste.
- Have plastic bags for trash and contaminated items.
- Use old towels lined with cotton handkerchiefs or muslin if you don't have disposable diapers (use plenty of Vaseline or thick antiseptic baby cream, you don't want diaper rash).
- Use disposable masks and gloves for tasks involving any risk of cross-infection.
- Burn paper • not plastic.
- Use a candle flame to sterilize needles, tweezers, and scissors before using on another person.
- Sanitize dishes, clothes, toys etc. in the sun.
- Go outside—fresh air is a healthy option.

- Compost all kitchen scraps.
- Cover your water supply and food.
- Isolate the sick from the healthy.
- Be sure to ventilate your space.
- Do not cross contaminate food or water.
- Ladies • a sea sponge is an excellent alternative if you run out of Tampax or sanitary napkins. You can use and then rinse and re-use. Remember to cut to size. (Sea sponges are sold at Home Depot.)

The toilet

More than likely during an emergency you will be unable to use your toilet facilities. This can be a bigger problem in the city than it can in the suburbs or countryside. There, you may have the option to use the great outdoors. If you have your own backyard you can dig a hole. If you live in a condo with no private space maybe you can get a group of you together to make collective arrangements.

A hole in the ground

Dig a hole in the ground as big around as a post hole digger and about as deep as your wrist (no deeper because more than six inches beneath the surface there are no bacteria to decompose the waste) You could probably put hundreds of holes in even a small backyard. They only need to be about an inch apart. After each use cover with a handful of earth. When the hole is reasonably full, (please use your common sense) cover it over. Burn the toilet paper. Please remember that if you are close to a water source, such as a well or a stream, dig your latrines at least 200 feet away!

Apartment dwellers

You're on the 26th floor of an apartment in the centre of town. Your power and water goes out. First thing—don't flush your toilet. Empty the water from the cistern into containers. It's clean and you may need it. Ensure that your emergency kit (you know, the one with the backpack size camping stove, the food supplies, water filter, blanket and first aid kit!) includes bottled water. You will have to carry your water a long way, it makes sense to have done the hard work while the elevator was working.

Using a bucket as a toilet

Another piece of advance planning is one you would not regret in an emergency. Acquire a 5-gallon bucket (or similar container, even an empty ammo can would work—use your imagination!). You can use it for storing stuff in, shoes, cleaning products, toys, anything. And get yourself a sack of sawdust or cedar chips, both should be available from a pet store. If space is at a premium disguise the sawdust by putting it inside a soft footstool, or incorporate it into a piece of furniture. Then in an emergency you can follow these instructions:

- Line the bucket with a refuse sack.
- Use the bucket.
- After each use, add a handful of dry sawdust (cedar works best) and mix it in.
- The sawdust soaks up the urine and dries up the fecal matter.
- When the bucket is full, take it outdoors, dig shallow trench (no more than six inches deep) and empty the contents into the trench. Cover with earth and let it compost.

- If you have no way to dig a trench, remove the bag and leave it far from inhabited areas. Be a good neighbor.

Handy tips

- Phone book pages make excellent toilet paper!

If you have no paper, sit over a bucket of water and splash your backside—like a French bidet! Always wash your hands. Personal hygiene is vitally important!

Tom's toilet

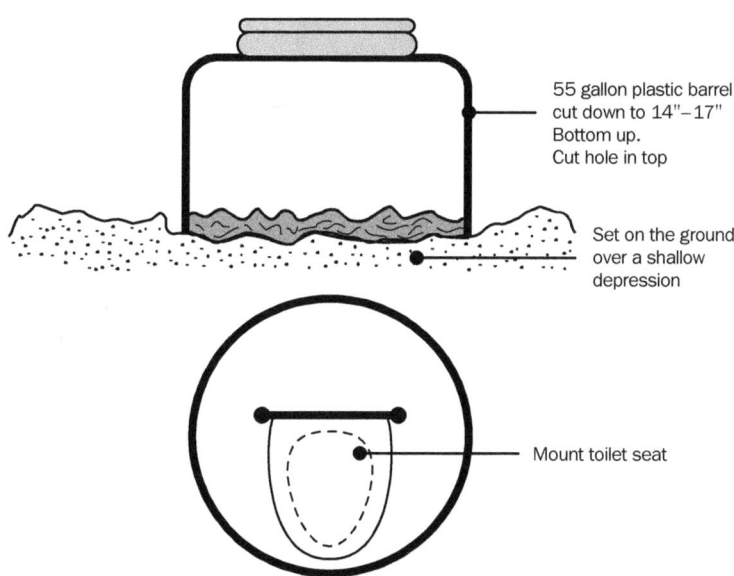

55 gallon plastic barrel cut down to 14"–17" Bottom up. Cut hole in top

Set on the ground over a shallow depression

Mount toilet seat

Survival tip ▶▶ Phone books are a great substitute for toilet paper.

Emergency first aid

"Your knowledge could save a life. Take CPR and a first aid course!"

Susan Conniry & Tom Beasley

Dealing with any sort of medical problem in an emergency is fraught with problems

If you have longstanding medical issues or disabilities you need to plan your emergency survival techniques now.

You need to talk to your medical practitioners and make sure you have every base covered. Delivery of medicines, medical equipment, and expert care may be seriously disrupted in the event of a local or national disaster. You can prevent yourself from becoming another casualty, or a drain on stretched resources, by planning ahead.

Training

If you are in good health, and especially if you have dependents, you owe it to yourself and your family to be prepared for a medical emergency. In a large disaster the emergency services will be overloaded and either slow or unable to respond. Your lack of knowledge could lead to a loss of life. Or your misguided attempts to help could make an injury worse. So take a class.

Get qualified in First Aid and CPR. If your area offers the initiative, learn AED (automated external defibrillation). These AED machines administer an electrical shock through the chest wall to the heart, and many businesses and public buildings such as airports are installing them. The equipment analyses the need of the victim and delivers the usage advice through computer technology. The American Red Cross and American Heart Association run courses in CPR and AED. Your local YMCA may also run classes.

Red Cross First Aid, CPR and AED classes are available for any age group and can be tailored to the needs of specific groups. Much of the training program is now available in Spanish. They also offer pet first aid classes, First Aid for Responding to Emergencies and Infant and Child first aid. Go to www.redcross.org and enter your zip code for more details of courses available near you.

For more intensive training, consider taking a **Wilderness First Responder** course. Visit: www.wildmed.com

If you are involved in an emergency and there are no qualified medical personnel available you should call 911 and ask for emergency medical services:

Waiting

While you are waiting you should ensure that the victim is neither chilled nor overheated.

' Do not move anyone unconscious or semi-conscious nor give them anything to eat or drink. If the victim is vomiting, place them on their side to prevent choking.

' If the victim faints, position them on their back and elevate their feet by about a foot. If the victim is having a seizure try and put something soft under their head but stay clear of thrashing which may injure you.

Bleeding

' If there is serious bleeding apply pressure with a clean absorbent cloth, or your fingers. If this cloth is soaked, add another. Don't remove the first as it will remove any clotting that may have occurred. If the bleeding doesn't stop, and you can do so, raise the wound above the level of the heart.

' If the bleeding stops, clean the wound gently with soap and water to remove debris. Squirting the liquid works better than rubbing.

' If the bleeding does not stop add an Ace bandage. If this fails, or if you have no bandage, apply continuous durect pressure.

- If a body part has been torn off wrap it in a clean dressing and place in a plastic bag but do not freeze as this destroys the tissues.
- Do not remove an object impaled in a wound. Leave this to the experts.

Burns

Burns come in three degrees from the least severe (first) to the most dangerous (third). Third degree burns require immediate medical attention as they destroy all layers of skin and some or all of the underlying fat, muscles, bones or nerve tissue. The burn will look black or brown and the tissues underneath may appear white. Any burn larger than the size of a hand could be life-threatening. With burns remember: never use ice on anything other than small superficial burns as it causes body heat loss. Cool burns with water or a cool, wet cloth. Cover burns to prevent infection but bandage loosely. Do not apply anything.

- Chemical burns • Should be flushed with water until the emergency medical services arrive.
- Electrical burns • Don't touch the victim until you know the power is off. Prevent the victim from becoming cold and use caution as spinal injuries may have occurred.

Poison

Call your poison center or emergency medical services immediately if you suspect someone of taking poison. Signs of poison include:

- Nausea.
- Vomiting.
- Diarrhoea.
- Chest or abdominal pains.

- Difficulty breathing.
- Changes in consciousness.
- Seizures.
- Burns around the lips and mouth.

You can be poisoned in four ways: inhalation (breathing it), ingestion (eating it), absorption (through the skin) and injection (bites and needles).

Self-reliance solutions—and preventions

Stay calm.

If your victim has breathed in a poison get them to fresh air as soon as possible. If they have poison on the skin take off any clothing that the poison touched and rinse their skin with running water for 15 to 20 minutes. If poison is in their eyes, rinse with running water for 15–20 minutes.

If they have eaten or drunk poison you are dependent upon medical assistance so you will have to access your local Poison Prevention Center. 1-800-222-1222 is the central switchboard if it or your telephone is still working. Have details of the poison and your victim ready when you call. If vomiting is recommended you will need to have an emetic such as syrup of ipecac, available in your first aid kit.

In an emergency situation stay away from places where poisonous creatures may be hiding. They won't really bother you unless you bother them. Remember the basics, dark basements and attics may house snakes or spiders. If you get bitten, wash the wound and keep your bite below your heart. do not: cut the wound or apply a tourniquet. do: Stay still. If anyone in your home is bee-sting allergic keep an epi-pen or your doctor prescribed medication with you at all times.

In an urban emergency rats and other feral animals such as dogs, cats, raccoons, skunks, foxes and bats may be disturbed. Even domestic animals may act oddly. Stay away from them. If you are bitten you will need to seek emergency attention promptly if you suspect rabies (drooling, partial paralysis, unusually quiet or irritable). If the wound is small, wash it with soap and water and apply antibiotic (check for known allergies). If large, control the bleeding as outlined above. Remember what the animal looked like and where you last saw it.

Natural and homeopathic medicines

This is a complex subject and not one that should be embarked upon during an emergency. There are many credible alternative medical treatments and homeopathic remedies as well as many positive endorsements for self-healing techniques derived from yoga and meditation. People who have studied these techniques will find many of the practices they have learned about will prove useful in a first response survival scenario. You are encouraged to learn more about this fascinating area of self-reliance.

Advance planning

There are a number of things you can do before an emergency. You can learn about the types of emergency situations most likely to strike you in your area by checking out your local county website or library. Discover whether there is a plan of action—whether you chose to use it or not is your choice but you should be aware of what the plans are. Your community may have a warning system in place for some types of emergency, i.e. TV, radio broadcast, siren, reverse 911 callling etc.

You know that in an emergency you will be hungry for information. Get yourself a battery or wind-up radio in case the TV goes down or you are stranded outside. And because we never know where we will be in an emergency we should plan things ahead with our family. Here are some suggestions for your family's preparedness plan.

- Discuss as a family the nature of possible emergency events.
- Discuss how you would respond to each type of emergency.

- Draw a floor plan and mark as many possible escape routes as possible and practise evacuating through them. (You may want to reconsider jumping through windows.)

- Find out how to turn off water, gas and electricity at the main switches. Do not attempt to reconnect your own gas supply when the emergency ends.

- Select a family member, out of state maybe, to act as a central liaison post. If you are separated you can relay messages through them in order to reunite your family.

- Consider how you would have to use your home, work or cell phone, if the networks are still working. Teach children how to make emergency, local and long distance calls from home, from a pay phone and from a cell phone. Leave numbers of emergency contacts and family in the home, in your wallet, in the children's school back packs.

- Pick five meeting places, two close to your home, three outside your neighbourhood in case you can't get back home. List these in the order you will try them on the same sheet of paper as the phone numbers.

- Tell your family members to listen to the radio.

- List and carry the names and numbers of family doctors, important medical information and the names and serial numbers of medical equipment such as pacemakers. Carry color photographs of other family members in case you get separated.

- Carry identification, credit cards, small notes in cash and photocopies of important documents such as household insurance. It is a good idea to have photocopies of all of these documents and cards held by your emergency contact out of state as you may lose everything and duplicates will make dealing with the aftermath a great deal easier.

- You will need spare sets of house and car keys. Work out where best to keep them in advance.

- Keep original family records in a fireproof/waterproof safe.

- Whatever or wherever you are, if you have kept the items from the emergency packs given at the end of this book you should be in good shape to deal with many emergency situations. Many needs will be basic such as tools, fire-making equipment, bleach, duct tape, needle and thread, warm clothes, toilet paper, trash bags, box-cutters, knives, etc. Make sure you have them someplace easy to find and grab if you are forced to leave in a hurry.

- Don't forget your pets. Make sure their shots are up to date, they are wearing ID and rabies tags, they have 2 weeks supply of food, clean bowls, etc. Keep their veterinary paperwork with you as most animal shelters do not allow pets without proof of vaccination.

- Turn off sensitive electrical equipment such as computers, VCR,s and television as well as major appliances, this will help to prevent power surges when electricity is restored. Don't call 911 for updates on power outages, listen to news stations for updates.

- Remember you will feel shocked after a traumatic incident. A good way to deal with this is to remain active and volunteer to help other victims. Children may wish to talk about it, often repeating stories over and over. Listen to them and encourage them to get involved in the rebuilding process: making cards, baking cookies, etc for emergency services personnel, etc.

Lists

"Attending your workshop, reading your book, I already feel better, less helpless and better equipped to survive, as well as able to help those around me. Thanks!"

Allyson, El Cajon, California

The dynamics of survival

We all have a basic survival instinct. We stay alive day in and day out by adhering to the rules—shelter, water, fire and food. A survival situation is a perceived condition. It is merely your conditioned comfort zone and its boundaries being moved. See your survival as a personal challenge. You can live without electricity. You can live without central heat. Using your brain, knowledge and your two hands a human can adapt to any situation. Turn it into a game. Instead of taking the easy way out present yourself with a challenge to overcome instead of something that will defeat you. Survival is everyone getting through. Focus your attention on the weakest link. Survival is beyond community; rather it is tribal. A tribe is a group of people with equal skills. Take away one member of the tribe and anyone else can pick up the slack. Organize your resources and your responses to a group of eight or less. Use your instincts—the animal within!

Pocket pouch

The pocket pouch is a small leather pouch that remains in your pocket at all times. Its contents may vary but this is what's in ours:

2 Benadryl capsules (for allergic reactions).
2 Maglite bulbs—Same size as your flashlight.
2 U.S. quarters.
8p nail.
A very small flat file.
Artificial sinew—Dental floss is a good substitute. It's waterproof and strong.
Basket Needle—That's a big needle.
Bic lighter (wrap a hair tie or elastic band around it).
Bobby pin.
Brass wire wrapped on a metal sewing machine bobbin. • Use Christmas wreath wire from a craft store.
Button.
Chap stick.
Ear plugs.
Magnesium fire starter.
P-38 can-opener—The army version, it's about an inch long.
Seam ripper—From a sewing or craft store.
Sewing needles (glovers' needles) for sewing leather.
Small flat screw driver.
Three fish hooks.
Toe nail clippers—They cut light wire, dental floss etc.
"Uncle Bill's" tweezers—Available in sport goods stores.

Fanny pack

Second item in the series of three. Not always carried but goes with the big backpack.

The fanny pack contains:

50 feet of 550 cordage—Military surplus or sportsman catalog. Made up of 7 strands which can be unraveled for lighter uses.
6' of flexible plastic tubing—$3/8"$—basically it's a giant drinking straw for your solar still.
6 × 6 6mil plastic sheet (clear)—Home Depot. A shower curtain will work if it's very light colored or clear.
Ace bandage.
Bandanna.

Boonie hat—Broad-brimmed sun hat that protects ears and neck. Military surplus stores.
Compass.
Dark cotton work gloves (insect sprayed).
Dust mask—Respro mask from www.respro.com is best.
Eye wash cup.
Goggles with extra dark lenses.
Iodine crystals—Sporting goods store.
Liquid soap—Will serve more purposes than anti-bacterial handwash, like lubing things.
Maglite flashlight (AA size)—keep on a lanyard.
Metal spoon—Serves many purposes, make sure it's a strong one.
One large oval carabiner.
Playtex rubber gloves.
Rechargeable AA batteries.
Safety pins.
Saw blades—Metal and wood versions from power tool it work well.
Sea sponge (feminine hygiene). For internal use. You may prefer to pack a few strips of terry towelling to wash'n'wear alternately. Pack extra safety pins.
Skull cap (like motorcycle riders wear).
Small sharpening stone.
Snakebite kit—Drugstore version. Be advised, they're not that great and Tom doesn't carry one now.
Sponge (for water gathering).
Toothbrush.
Tuna fish can—Empty 6 ozs can. 101 uses: digging, cooking, as a cup, a lamp base.
Washcloth.

Backpack

Being prepared to go mobile is always important. A backpack is like having your house on your back.

Contents: (this is our list—you may want other items)

·22 rifle.
100 feet of 550 cordage.
2 bandanas – Use them as a handkerchief, a potholder and, a whatever.
20 lb breakdown child's hunting bow—WalMart or any sporting goods store should have one. Remember to practice. You can use sharpened small sticks, or even pencils as arrows.

- 70 oz. (or larger) Camelbak—This is a water back pack with a straw to your mouth.
- 96 oz. Collapsible Nalgene water bottle.
- Bo staff – This is a martial arts stick. You'll need to find a specialist store. Tom has his drilled with holes which he uses to create bird traps and has given it a rubber tip to give better traction and silence the tapping noise it can make on rock.
- Boot liner—fleece.
- Boots—sturdy.
- Broad-brimmed fur felt hat with chin strap—Sporting goods or cowboy store. Felt sheds water and keeps the sun off.
- Compression bandage— A Kotex would do.
- Compression sacks (2)—From a sports or camping store. These bags squeeze air out of bulky items such as sleeping bags or clothes to save space.
- Ensolite pad—One of those sleeping pads available from a camping store such as rei or Sears. The dense foam can be cut up and used for padding.
- Expedition weight fleece long john underwear—top and bottom.
- Fleece balaclava.
- Fleece coat.
- Fleece mittens.
- Fleece pants.
- Fleece sleeping bag.
- Gaiters—Prevents stuff like snow, water and stones from getting in your boots.
- 1 qt. Nalgene wide mouth water container.
- Internal frame pack.
- Large safety pin—and some small ones.
- Large scarf—Get the regulation Army issue scarf. It's a multi-purpose item that can swathe your head and neck, double up as clothing, a bandage, a papoose, a sheet, a carrying device – almost anything you can think of.
- Leather belt—It's to hold your pants up. Yep, you'll lose weight surviving and you need to keep your hands free for important stuff.
- Leather gloves—Protect your hands from cuts and bites.
- Metal can with a removable metal handle—
- Military coat liner—lightweight nylon—Available from catalog or supplier like:

ww.sports www.sportsmansguide.com

Military pant liner—lightweight nylon—Available as for coat liner.

Mosquito head net—Sporting goods store.

Nylon shorts—Durable and they dry fast.

Nylon windbreaker.

Plastic sheet—6' × 6'—for solar still.

Poncho—Nylon rain poncho.

Poncho liner (lightweight nylon insert)—Military version is quilted for extra warmth. Tom says he's sewn two together and stuffed with leaves (wet or dry) to provide shelter and warmth.

PVC raincoat—top (with hood) and bottom—100% water-proof and very cheap. Resist the temptation to pay more for a fancy one!

Sand water filter tube (end of water bed tube).

Small day pack.

Socks—fleece.

Solar battery charger.

Space blankets (2).

Tent fly (for debris gathering).

Triangle bandage.

U.S. Forest Service Fire tent—This is the fire shelter that forest fire-fighters use if they get caught in the blaze. You curl up in it and wait for the flames to pass over you. You probably don't need one if you live in wetlands.

Washcloth.

Wasp spray.

Wool gloves—For warmth.

Car pack

This pack goes to work with you. It goes in your car. It is designed in case you're stranded and have to walk back home.

00 steel wool—For fire making.
9 volt battery—Same thing.
Ace bandage.
Aspirin.
Band-Aids.
Bandana.
Baseball type hat.
Benadryl.
Bic lighter.
Book for reading.
Can of tuna.
Candle.
Chapstick.
Cordage.
Cotton work gloves.
Extra eyeglasses.
Flashlight.
Knife.
Lard.
Large plastic trash bag.
Liquid iodine.
Map (several designated meeting places and routes of travel).
Money—small bills.
P-38 can-opener.
Pliers.
Raincoat.
Soap.
Sunglasses.
Throwing stick
Tuna can.
Walking shoes.
Warm long underwear.
Water.
Wool blanket.
Wool hat.

Long-term ideas

"Jar your thinking" list

·22 bullets.
10 gallon metal trash cans with lids.
Back scratcher.
Barbecue grill.
Bicycle.
Bicycle pump.
Bleach.
Books.
Bug spray.
Camp stove.
Chain saw.
Chlorine.
Clothespins.
Dog leashes.
Drinking alcohol.
Drop spindle for spinning wool.
Empty containers.
Extension cords.
Fire extinguisher.
Firewood.
Fly swatters.

Funnels.
Games.
Garden seeds.
Grain grinders.
Gun cleaning kit.
Lantern wicks.
Lanterns.
Maps.
Moving blankets.
Musical instruments.
Old clothes.
Paper.
Pens and pencils.
Phone books.
Pillows.
Push pins.
Rolls of plastic sheeting.
Rubber boots.
Sand.
Scissors.
Sewing supplies.
Shovels, rakes, garden hose.
Sling shot.
Smoking pipe.
Spray bottles.
Stuffed animals for the kids.
Sweaters.
Tent.
Tire repair kit.
Tobacco.
Toilet plunger.
Twine.
Wagon.
Whistle.
Wool blankets.

Tools

Awl.
Axe.
Baling wire.
Bolt cutters.
Box cutter.
Broom.
Chain.
Chisels.
Clamps.
Clipboard.
Clippers.
Come-along.
Crescent wrench.
Digging bar.
Duct tape.
Dustpan.
Ear plugs.
Electrical tape.
Eye protection.
Files.
Fireplace tools.
Floor mop.
Glue.
Hacksaw.
Hammers.
Hand drill and bits.
Hand pump.
Hatchet.
Heavy gloves.
Ladder.
Measuring tape.
Nails.
Pipe cement.
Pipe wrench.

Pitch fork.
Pliers.
Post hole digger.
Propane torch.
Punch.
PVC pipe.
Rags.
Rake.
Rasp.
Roofing cement.
Rope.
Rubber gloves.
Sandpaper.
Saw.
Screwdrivers.
Shovel.
Splitting mall.
Stapler.
Trowel.
Various screws, nuts and bolts.
Vice.
Vice grips.
WD-40.
Window screen.
Wire cutters.

Car parts

Antifreeze.
Battery.
Brake fluid.
Bulbs.
Clutch fluid.
Fan belts.
Fuel cans.
Fuses.
Hoses.
Jack.
Oil.
Spare tire.
Spark pugs.
Transmission fluid.
Wood block.
Wrench.

Kitchen

Bags.
Barbecue grill.
Bowls.
Colander.
Cups.
Cutlery, i.e. knife, fork, spoon.
Cutting board.
Cutting knives.
Dish rack.
Dish soap.
Dish towels.
Dish towels.
Dutch oven.
Foil.
French press.
Manual can opener.
Measuring cups and spoons.
Paper towels.
Plastic bags.
Pot holders.
Potato peeler.
Pots, pans, lids.
Recipe books.
Scrubby pads.
Spatula, large spoon.

Strainer.
Tea ball.
Tea kettle.
Timer.
Tongs.
Trash can with lid.
Various storage containers.
Wok.

Garden

Baskets.
Bird netting.
Bow saw.
Chicken wire.
Clippers.
Hand trowel.
Hand weed sickle.
Have-a-heart trap.
Hose.
Machete.
Nozzle.
Trash burning barrel.
Watering can.
Yard sprayer.

Medical cabinet

In any survival situation, it is imperative that you exercise care. The simplest things can easily escalate into a life-threatening situation. Preparation is essential and in some cases very easy to do. If you know you require certain life-preserving medicines keep them handy: in your car, your purse, your computer case, your home, or at a friend's house. If you use contact lens ensure you have spares and adequate cleaning solutions.
If you wear spectacles keep cheap replacements with you.

Preparedness

Get your vaccinations current: Hepatitis A and Tetanus.
Take a First Aid course.
Take a CPR course.
Take a Wilderness First Responder Course.
Stock up on special prescription medications, i.e. insulin.

Consider including these items in your own home medical kit:

3" × 5" cards.
Ace bandages.
Adhesive tape.
Analgesics.
Antacids.
Antibiotics—Keep them current. Check expiry dates on all medications.
Anti-diarrhoea.
Antihistamines.
Asthma medication.
Band-Aids.
Chapstick.
Cold packs.
Crutches.
Epinephrine—The epi-pen should be with anyone who is subject to anaphylactic shock. As they have been known to malfunction a phial and syringe alternative should be available and kept very, very close by.
Eye drops.
Hemorrhoidal treatment.
Hand lotion.
Hot water bottle.
Iodine.
Laxatives.
Lice medication.
Oil of cloves.
Pen and pencil.
Razor blades.
Rubbing alcohol.
Sanitary napkins/Tampons.
Scissors.
Sheets for bandages.
Skin medication, i.e. calamine lotion, anti-fungal creams.
Smelling salts—ammonia.
Soap.
Splints.
Syrup of Ipecac.
Thermometer.
Vitamins.
Watch.

Areas to consider

Geriatric.
Pediatric: diapers, child-strength medicines.
Childbirth.
Dental.

Personal hygiene

Items to consider:

Anti-microbial soap.
Baby strength products.
Conditioner.
Dental floss.
Feminine hygiene.
Razor blades.
Shampoo.
Sunscreen.
Toothbrush.
Toothpaste.
Towels.
Washcloth.

Miscellaneous

Things to consider:

·22 rifle.
Animal husbandry.
Barrels
Beer and wine making kits.
Blacksmithing.
Bow and arrows.
Charcoal.
Cistern for rain water.
Compost pile.
Disposable brushes.
Engine repair.
Farming.
Fishing.
Gun cleaning kit.
Hand trowel.
Hibachis.
Hunting.
Kerosene.
Lumber.
Permanent markers.
Plywood.
Potato/corn chips for lamp.
Propane.
Propane torch.
Sand bags.
Sleeping pads.
Solar still.
Wind-up alarm clock.

Pets

Things to consider:

Bowls.
Food.
Leashes.
Medicine.
Fleas.
Parasites, Fleas.
Sleeping.
Toys.

Directory

"You took away the fear, gave folks simple ideas in regards to survival skills and preparation. Thank you for working with us."

Division Chief Bob Krans (retired)

Poway Safety Services

Catalogs/Websites:

Cheaper than Dirt
    1-888-625-3848   www.cheaperthandirt.com

Real Goods
    1-800-762-7325   www.realgoods.com

Provident Pantry
    1-800-999-1863   www.beprepared.com

The Sportsman's Guide
    1-800-888-5222   www.sportsmansguide.com

Smoky Mtn Knife Works
    1-800-251-9306   www.SmKwKnife.com

Major Surplus
    1-800-441-8855   www.MajorSurplusNSurvival.com

Campmor
    1-800-226-7667   www.campmor.com

Cabelas
    1-800-237-4444   www.cabelas.com

Recreational Equipement, Inc.
    1-800-426-4840   www.rei.com

Adventure 16
    (619) 283-2362   www.adventure16.com

C. Crane Company
    1-800-522-8863   www.ccrane.com

Native Seed Search
    1-520-622-5561   www.nativeseeds.org

Crazy Crow
    1-800-786-6210   www.crazycrow.com

Sierra Trading Post
    1-800-713-4534   www.sierratradingpost.com

Books

Author	Title
U.S. Army Survival Guide	U.S. Government
Werner, Thuman & Maxwell	Where There is No Doctor.
Muray Dickson	Where There is no Dentist
Tom Brown, Jr.	Wilderness Survival
Tom Brown, Jr.	City and Suburban Survival
John and Jerrie McPherson	Primitive Wilderness Living and Survival Skills
Eric A. Weiss	Wilderness and Travel Medicine
Jeffrey Isaac	First Responder Outward Bound
Tory Peterson	Peterson Field Guides
Michael Moore	Medicinal Plant Guides
Paul Tawrell	Camping and Wilderness Survival
Ragnar Benson	Do-it-yourself Medicine
USG Field Manual Survival—FM21/76	
Skipper Clarke	Creating Complete Food Storage
Thomas Elpel	Participating in Nature
Paul Campbell	Native Skills of California
Paul Campbell	2 oz Backpacker

Videos

Hoods Woods	www.survival.com/

Manufacturers and supplies

Iodine Crystal Supplier: Granny's Country Store,
   p.o. Box 684, Silver Star, mt 59751-0684 (406) 287-3605

Katadyn Water Filters • 1-800 760-7942 | www.katadyn.net

Tandy Leather • 1-800-433-3201 | www.tandyleather.com

Whispering Bear (leather and supplies) • (718) 351-6768

Food Reserves • 800-944-1511 | www.foodreserves.com

AccuSharp (Knife and Tool Sharpeners) • 800-553-5129

No endorsements are implied or give, this list is for reference only.

The authors

"Concerned citizens can acquire basic skills and knowledge and make preparations. The resulting increase in their confidence itself is a tremendous asset."

Susan Conniry & Tom Beasley

Biography of Susan Conniry and Tom Beasley

Susan acquired her BA from San Diego State University, a credential in physical education from Grossmont Community College and has been teaching for 25 years. Her political experience ranges from that of a citizen activist, to a member of the Planning Commission for the City of Santee, and Chairman of the Board for the Assessment Appeals Board for the County of San Diego.

Tom Beasley has 30 years experience in backpacking and has been awarded 11 certificates from the renowned Tom Brown Jr.'s Tracking, Nature and Wilderness School. He is a graduate of National Outdoor Leadership School (NOLS) and is a certified Wilderness First responder.

In 2000, Susan founded Backyard Tourist, Inc. a non-profit educational organization (www.backyardtourist.com) as a means to pursue her work through the teaching of classes that emphasize man's delicate balance with nature.

Since 2001, Susan and Tom have provided a unique interactive program, The Coyote Youth Project, an environmental edcucational program that combines afterschool experiences with standards-based curriculum for high school students in San Diego County. The program is funded through grants and private donations.

The focus of all Tom and Susan's work has been teaching nature awareness in various environments by creating an understanding of the need for simpler living in order to reduce humanity's impact on the Earth. However, in 1997, the increased potential of disasters from wild-fires, earthquakes and El Nino flooding raised the need for teaching urban dwellers about disaster preparedness. Knowing that emergency services personnel are often understaffed and under-budgeted, they undertook the unique approach to disaster preparedness by adapting wilderness skills into an urban environment and began teaching concerned citizens techniques that utilize resources in their immediate environment. They teach communities how to **"take care of themselves."**

§ 10 | NOTES

§ 10 | NOTES

§ 10 | NOTES

§ 10 | NOTES

§ 10 | NOTES

§10 | NOTES

www.ingramcontent.com/pod-product-compliance
Lightning Source LLC
LaVergne TN
LVHW051841080426
835512LV00018B/3011